Passing through Grief

Move beyond coping with grief to recover fully and create a new wholehearted life.

By Natalia Volz

Passing through Grief
Move beyond coping with grief to recover fully and create a new wholehearted life.

Published by Wholehearted Life Publishing
P.O. Box 134
Swarthmore, PA 19081

ISBN: 978-0998419503

Cover design by Jim Saurbaugh, JS Graphic Design

laws and regulations, both advertising and all other aspects of doing business in the United States or any other jurisdiction, is the sole responsibility of the purchaser or reader.

Dedicated to

Sean, Alena and Sarah,
and to all who have experienced deep loss.

Table of Contents

Acknowledgements

With deep gratitude:

To my beautiful children, Sarah, Alena and Sean, for cheering me on as I followed my passion of starting my own business and as I wrote this book. I know it's been a scary ride at times since Dad died. I am proud of all of you for continuing to grow into amazing young adults through life's adversities. I love you immensely!

To my parents, Cynthia and Anatole Bredikin, for always loving me and being there for me during the toughest of days;

To my sister, Tatiana Bredikin, for believing in me, patiently listening to me through all my sadness and fears, and loving me unconditionally always;

To my entire family for being supportive and caring always;

To Jim Palmer, my business coach – this book never would have happened without your belief in me, your guidance, and occasional kick in the pants;

To my very good friend and my greatest cheerleader, Deirdre Bernstein, for believing in me and this book when I didn't believe in myself;

To Eils Lotozo and Gamal Sherif for walking with me on this journey of creating the lives we truly desire. I could not have gotten this far without you;

To my friend Maria Mooney, for help with editing and encouragement;

To my dear friend Charlene, for your openness to being my first "client" and then referring friends to me afterward, and for your continuous love;

To John W. James and Russell Friedman and the Grief Recovery Institute for teaching me how to move through my own grief and teaching me how to help others;

To Christy Whitman and Quantum Success Coaching Academy for teaching me how to create the life I desire and training me how to coach others in doing the same;

To Barbara Stanny, who started me, in her Sacred Success Retreat, on the road to realizing my dream of helping others through grief and who taught me to take the first little step and then keep taking consistent, small steps to reach my goals;

To Holisticare Hospice for giving me the opportunity to do the work I love in a supportive hospice setting;

And to my editor, Ann Deiterich, for making this book a reality through her amazing editing.

With much love,
Natalia

Preface

I faced widowhood at an early age. My children became fatherless long before they should have. It was an intense and immense loss.

I struggled with grief and struggled longer than was necessary. Through my own struggles and trial and error, and the help of some grief experts, I learned a lot about the steps needed to be able to move forward in life again. From what I learned, I wanted to guide others with their own personal journeys through grief.

That said, there is no exact blueprint. There is no exact timeline. Grief is as individual as every other aspect of our lives, our personalities, ourselves.

The result of my own experience, my research, and my eventual training was the creation of my company, Passing Through Grief. I have guided many individuals through grief, and I have facilitated many groups, guiding individual group members through recovering from grief.

My goal in writing this book is to help you better understand grief and the grieving process while guiding you through the steps you need to take to recover from grief and remake your life. There are certain steps we all must take as we move through grief; however, the size and timing of those steps is highly personal.

Throughout the book, I have shared my own story in depth. While there is a certain catharsis in that (and as you go through the steps, you will learn the value of journaling and writing about your own feelings), I certainly do not intend this book to be autobiographical. I share what I do so you understand my experience and also can draw many parallels between what I went through as a result of death and loss and what you are experiencing or have experienced.

Whether from prolonged illness or unexpectedly sudden, death and loss bring grief. It doesn't actually matter how the loss you experienced occurred. The result is pain. That pain is what brought me to where I am in my life, and it is that pain that likely brought you into these pages.

In sharing parts of my story throughout the book, I want to let you know in advance that I have altered the font to make it more readable. I share my story to let you know that I have been there; I know the devastating pain of loss and grief. Most importantly, I share my story because I want you to know that you too can heal. You will not feel like this forever. I am living testament to that.

Regardless of the situation surrounding your own loss and feelings, I've learned that no matter how long it may take, there are steps to take to move through your grief and move beyond loss, so you can live wholeheartedly.

I hope you've noticed that I've repeatedly used the word "through" in regard to the grieving process. That is the one thing that is the same for all of us. In order to move forward and live wholeheartedly, you must move *through* it. You cannot circumnavigate grief and you cannot avoid it. With this book, I hope to help you through this journey, difficult as it is, because I know the healing that is on the other side.

Preface

Introduction
What No One Tells You about Loss and Grief

"The best thing one can do when it's
raining is to let it rain."
~ Henry Wadsworth Longfellow

It doesn't come in a neat package.

There are no clear instructions.

It's not the same for everyone, so your grief does not look like my grief.

There are no timetables for grief.

There is no straight line out of grief. It is all over the place. Two steps forward, five steps back, one step forward, three steps forward, two back. Totally unpredictable.

You can cope alone, but you can't heal alone. You can't do it alone and completely recover.

Your friends don't have a clue how to help you through it. Many people will be scared of you... like you are contagious.

Some of your closest friends will have to fall away. They won't be able to walk this walk with you. New friends you never expected will show up.

Your life will never get back to normal. You will have to create a new normal.

You have to take action to recover.

Grieving with All the Wrong Information

Are you "keeping busy" to try to get over the grief you feel since the death of someone you loved?

Our bodies, hearts, and minds are affected by grief and loss.

All that advice from friends and family saying:

- "Get busy" or
- "Move on" or
- "Try a hobby"…

… is wrong. Not helpful one bit! Keeping busy does not help us recover from the pain of the death of a loved one.

First, realize that grief is tough stuff. It is not meant for the weak, believe me. You are stronger than you may know at this point.

The effects of grief are real. It is not in your head, and you can't ignore grief or all the pain that arises due to your loss. It will pop out all over no matter how hard you try to cover it up. So stop trying. You can't cover it up and make it go away.

Honestly, there is only one way to get rid of grief: You must go through it.

Sorry, no alternatives. No ways around it. No way under it or over it. You must pass right through the center, through the muck, the agony, the horrendous feelings. Yep. Don't let anyone tell you otherwise. Grief must be experienced.

I tried coping with my grief for a year after my husband died, and I was still in pain. I couldn't figure out how to end my grief, so I got busy and tried to ignore it. But I couldn't ignore it. It popped up at the most inopportune times, like while in line at the grocery store, at my son's hockey game, watching TV, or while out for a walk through my town.

"Keeping busy" is exhausting … running and running until we drop. We go into overdrive running from the pain, but it is there again as soon as we stop. At night, when it's quiet, grief is waiting for you. We keep busy hiding how much we hurt, and we can barely function.

New clients often ask me, "How come this loss wasn't enough? My whole life now seems to be falling apart." They are sick, they are fighting with family and friends, they are losing their jobs on top of losing their loved ones, and they are getting in car accidents and injuring their bodies.

These things happen because they are not giving themselves the time and space to grieve completely and let the pain of grief out.

Yes, we must let grief pass through us, so we can recover and move on! Someone we cared deeply about is gone from us. We can't hear their voice. Touch them. They aren't here to help us. It is painfully devastating. Keeping busy will not take away that pain.

However, a better life is possible and meant for you. You are not meant to live a miserable life. This loss is horrible enough. You deserve to live wholeheartedly! But it is hard to quickly feel better. Others may not understand what it takes to move through the pain of your great loss.

I wish it were as easy as "keeping busy." I wish keeping busy could make your pain go away.

Keeping busy fills your time. Busyness makes others feel better about how you are doing, but at the end of the day, the pain is still there when all we do is keep busy. Keeping busy is exhausting, and you are probably already exhausted.

Keeping busy does not get out all of the emotions related to your loss. It does not get out all of the thoughts filling your head. It does not rid you of your guilt, regrets, fears, and disappointment over lost hopes, dreams, and expectations.

I wish more for you than keeping busy, trying to mask your pain. I wish for you to move through the pain of your incredible loss whether it is a death of a loved one or another loss.

Recovery Is Difficult, but Possible

It is possible for you to move forward, and there are tools for moving through the grief. However, it seems impossible to recover after the death of a loved one because you don't have the right information or the right vehicle for recovery. In fact, you were given all the wrong information, and with the vehicle and misinformation you have, recovery very well may be impossible.

If you are trying to go from New York to California and someone gives you the wrong directions, telling you to head east from New York into the Atlantic Ocean, it certainly seems impossible, especially when the vehicle you have is a car, not a boat. You are never making it to California that way!

This is why it seems impossible to recover from grief. You have the wrong directions and no vehicle for moving through it and arriving to a life you desire.

Have you been told:

- "Keep busy. That will make you feel better."
- "Be strong for _____. That will make you feel better."
- "Get out and have some fun. That will make you feel better."
- "Don't be sad. She's in a better place. Doesn't that make you feel better?"

Do any of these make you feel better?

If you have heard and believed any of these statements, then you have the wrong information for recovering from your grief and your loss. These statements may help you cope with grief, but you will not recover.

Coping is not good enough. Coping is surviving. It is not thriving. A life of coping is dull; it's living a gray life. I wish for you, like me, to return to a life full of color and aliveness.

My bet is you and your whole support system learned at a young age the wrong way to make it successfully through a devastating loss.

Then you experienced the devastating loss.

You tried everything you thought you knew – everything you had been taught – to get through it. Nothing made you feel better. So you are stuck. You are stuck in the pain. You are stuck in the confusion. You are stuck in isolation. And you now fear that there is no way out. You are just the person whose life is not meant to be happy now.

No! I challenge that belief. You and everyone else you know simply have the wrong information and the wrong vehicle. I will argue that it is entirely possible to recover after a death. In the example of getting from New York to California, I am going to point you in the right direction and give you the right vehicle. It's still a long journey. You will not get there overnight, but you will get there.

Recovery is possible and it is meant for you. You would not be reading this if you were not meant to recover.

Stop Acting ... Stop Pretending

Are you acting as if you have recovered or have you actually recovered from your loss and grief? I'm wagering it's the former.

I live in quite an unusual town for this day and age. Neighbors in our town know each other and reach out to help one another in need. So when my husband died, initially there was an outpouring of help. Our freezer was stocked with prepared meals. Our gardens were weeded and our lawn mowed. Rides were arranged for my children to get to their activities.

But I remember one month after my husband's death the feeling of grief settling in for a long visit, the despair and, even more, the feeling of isolation and loneliness.

Friends, neighbors, and colleagues cared. I could see it in their eyes when they saw me walking toward the bleachers at my son's lacrosse games. It pained them to see that I was suffering. Yet they didn't know what to say or do.

I began to work to hide my pain.

Each morning, I'd get my children off to school, then sit down at my computer in my home office working. Frequently I'd sob, my heart aching for my husband.

But I'd pull myself together to pick the kids up from school at 3:30. I'd see all the mothers who felt lost and scared about what to say to me. They preferred to keep their distance. I was learning now to act recovered.

As months went on, more people kept their distance. As I walked down the street, they would avert my eyes. If forced to converse, they would tell me I was so strong. They would tell me I was doing so well. I handled my loss with grace, they said.

I felt alone, lost, but I hid my pain and fears from them now. They liked it that way. I understood.

I knew how to stay inside when I couldn't hold myself together. I isolated more. I became most comfortable being alone. I'd literally prepare myself mentally and physically to go out of the house.

As the months turned into a year and then two, I felt more and more broken. I couldn't fix me. No one was able to fix me. The more time passed, the more broken I felt. The more embarrassed I felt about my inability to "get back to normal."

So I became a master at acting like I was back to my old self. But the pain was no less. My suffering was immense, but no one knew it anymore.

Are you like I was? Are you acting differently than you truly feel inside?

Acting recovered does not help us recover from the pain and suffering caused by our loss and our grief.

We have to break down the wall we hide behind to begin to recover. We have to let out the secret to someone that we have not truly recovered.

And this is frightening because we are so vulnerable when our wound of grief is open and raw. Yet we have to stop pretending, at least with one person whom we can trust.

Yes, in order to pass through grief we have to have our pain witnessed by another. Another who believes in our ability to one day recover, without their having to fix it for us. Another who validates our journey through grief and trusts us to find our way… to one day recover from our loss and our grief, to feel better, and then begin to remake our life.

Instead of pretending you have recovered, I know you can actually recover from the suffering you are experiencing in grief. I know you can recover fully, feel better inside, and have the opportunity to remake your life. A life you desire and deserve.

Chapter One:
His Death Was the Easy Part

"If you are going through hell, keep going."
~ Winston Churchill

His death, it turns out, was the easy part.

It was early Christmas morning. With three young children, we were already up and opening gifts. This year was unique: We were celebrating Christmas on the floor in our master bedroom. Peter, at this point, was unable to get out of bed. He was lifeless, though alive, in our bed. He had done his best to hold on until Christmas – a promise he had made me early in his diagnosis of pancreatic cancer.

"Just don't die between my birthday and New Year's Day. Too many holidays that will be ruined for the rest of our lives if you die then." I made this request when we learned in June that he had maybe six months to live. Pete promised.

The master bedroom was light, filled with the morning sun streaming through the eastern windows on that Christmas morning. Our queen-sized bed took up only part of the room but looked like a throne at this point with our king as its occupant. Even with his now thin physique – his usual husky one shrunken drastically from cancer – he still had a presence as large as a king and somehow as always he dominated the room.

So here we were Christmas Day, and he was hanging on for dear life. He was unresponsive. I had by now told him it was okay to go. I didn't want him to suffer one more day. But he was always a man of his word and very responsible. So Christmas morning he was with us … physically.

The excitement of Christmas with the kids in the room was not altogether gone even with their father barely present. It was as if he were sleeping through Christmas morning, uncharacteristic of him, but it seemed to get the kids through it. They were coping and protecting their gentle souls by pretending that all was almost normal.

The kids each gave him the final gifts they would ever give. Our son presented him a book and sweetly sat next to him on the bed reading the first chapter.

Our daughter gave him a pair of slippers and gently placed slipped them on his cold feet. Our younger daughter made him a picture in school and placed it carefully on the nightstand by his side.

After breakfast, my parents and siblings arrived. The kids opened gifts with them downstairs in the family room while I sat vigil next to Pete all day and night. His breathing was slowing.

Family came up one by one to say goodbye. I'd have brief breaks when they came up. However, I didn't need a break then. I felt so at peace. I felt prepared for him to go. We had talked about everything. Or so I thought at that time.

A week before Christmas, my father and I had helped Pete upstairs to bed, and he'd never come back down. He fought to make it through the holidays. Confused, frail, no longer eating or even drinking, speech gone, yet aware and determined, he held on to dear life. I stayed in the present. No thoughts of the future now.

> *I was prepared*
> *... or so I*
> *thought.*

I told him it was okay; he didn't have to keep his promise to live through the holidays. It was too hard watching him suffer. He grunted angrily when I told him to let go. Christmas Eve was the last time he was at all responsive. With his family over for our traditional Christmas Eve complete with a gingerbread-house-making contest, gift giving, and a delicious dinner for those downstairs, Peter lay very, very close to death upstairs with me by his side almost every minute.

December 26, 2010 was a beautiful evening. It started snowing early, a snowstorm brewing. I joked with the hospice nurse, "Leave it to Pete to die tonight." He always had to have a good story, and this would be a good one. It was peaceful. He was no longer suffering. The struggling was over for him. I told the kids before they headed to bed, "I don't think Dad will live through the night."

They each said goodbye to him one last time. I had soft music playing. I was told hearing is the last thing to go. A candle was lit and the lights were dim. I lay on the bed next to Pete where I had been for the last week. He was thin and a skeleton of his former self. Not sure why but I felt calm. I talked softly to him and read him prayers. I tired by midnight and began to doze off. He always joked that I could sleep through anything. I wanted to be awake when he left his body, but I couldn't keep my eyes open. I dozed off. I awoke at 1:20 a.m. His breathing had slowed to a breath every few seconds, then every five seconds, then seven. Then he took his last quiet breath and was gone. I waited to see if another breath would come. In the early morning of December 27, I kissed him goodbye and wished him a blessed journey into the next life.

I sat quietly alone with him for many minutes. I then woke my children to let them see him one last time, carrying them in one at a time. There was by now at least a foot of snow outside. I smiled at Pete's leaving on a night like this. It was so beautiful, yet not easy. That was Pete. He never claimed to be an easy husband, son, or friend, but he was an incredible person.

I thought I had just been through hell watching my strong husband suffer and face his death. Hell was over now, or so I thought.

After Death, Grief Enters

Like I said, it turns out death was the easy part.

Grief entered the picture.

Then the out-of-body experience began:

I saw a woman walking down the hall to wake her three children to inform them that their daddy had died.

She handled everything so calmly ... from caring for her children to planning the funeral.

She had energy those first few days after he died. With the help of family, she got the obituary written and submitted, she made all the funeral arrangements, friends told her she looked great at the funeral and after party. And she felt okay.

The first day with Pete gone, I am physically exhausted. I move, but like a robot. I do what has to be done to prepare for the funeral. People drop off meals, my parents and sister are there for my every need. My nephew, a young adult now, takes my son skiing for the day. My older daughter's friend takes her to the mall and they hang out at the house throughout the day, being silly as 13-year-old girls can be. My youngest quietly hangs close by me. Crying occurs mainly behind bedroom doors.

The out-of-body experience continues at the funeral. I always wondered how young wives made it through their husbands' funerals. Now I am the one with all eyes on me. "How is she doing this?" "She's so strong." "The poor kids. This is so tragic." A friend drops off a Valium for me to help me make it through the funeral. Running around getting everyone dressed and out the door on time, I forget to take it. At that point I am numb anyway. For the receiving line, I stand next to my husband's casket, seeing people I haven't seen in years. Hugging, talking briefly, feeling okay. And then the service starts.

The church is packed. I am told to walk down the aisle behind the casket. It feels surreal. I feel like I am walking down the aisle at my wedding but think how strange that it is actually my husband's funeral. And my three young children are walking with me behind their father's casket. How can this be my life? It cannot be real. The service is beautiful but does not feel real.

Afterward, everyone is invited back to our house. Friends from our community put on an incredible open house. Pete would have loved it. It's perfect. I am surprised that I feel fine. I don't feel sad. A lot of people come up to me crying and I comfort them. Some people cry, telling me that they feel bad that they have not been there for us. I tell them it's okay. I make them feel better. One person corners me and tells me he feels angry at Pete about unresolved issues from the past. I listen. My children run around with friends. They love it. It's a nice event. I feel surrounded by warmth and love. I go to bed feeling tired, but peaceful.

The next morning I wake and feel completely exhausted. I can barely move. My neighbor comes for coffee. I sit in my sweats staring blankly as she talks. I am unable to hear anything. She doesn't seem to notice. I am told to call if I need anything. I will not call. I do not know what I need.

My sister has flown in from Oregon, thank God. She's the person I am closest to in the whole world. She encourages me to listen to my body and rest as I need. I can barely get out of bed this first week. My body aches terribly. She makes sure the kids eat and get places they want and need to go. She intercepts calls and visitors. She listens to me, feeds me, cares for me.

Pete's funeral is on December 30. The following day, New Year's Eve, I am invited to a party. I can barely walk, but I decide to stop by. I crawl out of bed, get dressed, throw on some makeup, and go to the party. I stay an hour, see myself smiling and even laughing once. I see that everyone is watching me; I feel like I am on stage. No one suspects I will fall back in bed in an hour and not get out for a week.

One week to the day after Pete died, I wake up and decide I'd better get in the office to see if his clients need anything. I walk in and start answering the phone. Clients request jobs to be finished, then start sending new jobs.

I don't remember a lot throughout the first year. I'd get up in the morning, slip on sweats, and get the kids off to school. With little preparation or training, I'm now in charge of Pete's graphic design business. I head into his home office as soon as the kids leave and end up staying there for long hours managing a business I know little about.

The out-of-body experience continues. I have no idea who this person is that is doing this job.

She never learned anything about graphic design. She never had her own business. Her husband had his own business. She always admired his work.

She hires people to do the design. She meets with clients. Invoices jobs. Bids new jobs. Her days consist of working, sobbing, working, sobbing, crumbling on the floor hysterical, back up and working.

She has an occasional visitor. But they are rare. It has now been more than six weeks since her husband died.

Grief is so physical. In the beginning I feel like I have the flu. Maybe I do. My body continues to ache on and off for months. It feels heavy. My hips hurt whenever I walk. I feel old. I want to walk, I really want to run, run fast, run away, but my body doesn't cooperate. I feel stuck.

> Grief isn't just emotional. It's very, very physical.

I can't think about anything except the moment I am in. I feel in a fog much of the time. I am not thinking clearly. In fact, numerous times I find I leave the keys in the car and the car running when I've gone into a store. I feel scared when I come out and hear the car running. What is wrong with me? Never in my life was that something I would have done.

Bills pile up. I forget to pay things on time. I get a letter that my Internet may be turned off.

Who are my friends? There is my oldest friend. She makes me laugh when we talk no matter how grim my life looks. I love when I talk with her. But she could not be here for me when Pete was so sick. She can bring meals like others, but she can't stare my life in the face. She is too scared also. I protect her. I understand. She cannot handle my pain. We used to talk at least once a week. Once Pete got sick, it lessened. Pete died; it lessened again. We go weeks without talking.

Another friend has been there for me through it all. She brings meals, books, a needed chair, anti-anxiety pills. She shows up ready to take me out for a walk, hug me. And yet I am still all alone. I still cry alone. She senses when I am upset and calls to check on me. I call back when I am done bawling uncontrollably. No one can do this for me or even with me.

My sister checks in from across the country. Sometimes I cry so hard noises unfamiliar to me come out of me. I put the phone down on the bed, and she listens silently as I wail and groan. It slows, then stops. I feel lighter for a short time.

I am experiencing grief in all its power, and I don't even know it.

Coping Is All We Can Do in the Beginning

Coping. In the beginning coping with grief is all we can do. It's all we must do. Just cope. Aim to survive. Keep your nose above water … that's all you need for air, just your nose, the rest can be submerged. Just don't drop your nose under or you're done.

Coping is enough for the first six weeks. Often, friends are still bringing meals, or at least there are enough lasagnas or casseroles in the freezer from people who brought them during the first week. You weren't hungry anyway, so the lasagnas are there a month or more later when the kids are hungry.

I wish it were enough to cope for much longer because we cannot know exactly how long we need to do just that – cope. But that is not the world most of us live in. It is unfortunate how quickly employers require us to return to work. And it can be dangerous.

The Grief Recovery Institute conducted research on the effects of grief in the workplace. If we have not recovered from grief, our critical thinking is not functioning and we make poor decisions on the job. There is an inability to concentrate, focus and problem solve, or think long-term.

For many, when it is a loss of a special person they lived with or had a very close relationship with or someone they had an intense or lengthy relationship with, common feelings may include:

- numbness
- exhaustion or lack of energy
- temporary loss of memory
- confusion
- lack of focus and concentration
- problem-solving skills affected
- physical aching
- sleeping patterns disturbed
- eating patterns disturbed
- emotional roller coaster

For Jews in ancient times, when a significant person died, the mourners were cared for and not expected to do a single thing. The mourners sat low on a box signifying how they felt. Friends and community were responsible for visiting but not expected to speak to the bereaved. In fact, they were not allowed to talk to the bereaved unless spoken to first. They were simply required to bring food; not to eat the food, just bring the food for the family in mourning.

The bereaved wore black for an entire year, reminding the community that those grieving were not to be asked to do anything. At the one-year mark, the bereaved were instructed to return to living. But they had just spent a full year grieving.

Although I may not agree with putting a specific time limit on grief – it may take shorter or longer than a year – there is something I like about this ancient custom.

What you may not realize is that coping is your body's way of protecting you from the fact that you no longer have your special person. Your body naturally takes care of you. We simply have to learn to listen to it and trust it.

What Can You Do Now?

If you are in the first year of your loss, how can you cope? How can you care for yourself in a culture that does not recognize the necessary time for grieving?

1) **Accept help that people offer.** This is not easy for many of us. But it is crucial at this time! Consciously choose to accept help.

   When you think of things that need to be done, write them down under "notes" on your smartphone or on a note pad. When people say, "Let me know how I can help," it is not helpful because we cannot think clearly or about the future when we are in the beginning of the grief process, so we don't know what we will need. We're also afraid to ask in fear that we will be rejected right when we already feel rejected due to the loss we've experienced. We are very sensitive to rejection when grieving because our brain knows we need others to survive, so we are ultra-alert to who can actually help.

2) **Create a list of important people to help you**. Make two lists of the caring people in your life. One list of "Be-ers" and a second list of the "Do-ers." (In the days after my husband died, the phrase I heard repeated was, "Call if you need anything." While that offer is generous, it's hard to know what to ask for and when to take advantage of it. That's where the list of people in your life becomes critical.)

Be-ers: The people in your life who are able to listen to you without judgement, can sit quietly and take your lead, believe that you have within what it will take to heal from this trauma. They are the ones who bring you little thoughtful gifts like flowers, calming music, tea.

Do-ers: The people in your life who love to do and be busy. These are the people who can pick up your mail every day and deliver it to your front step and would love to do so. They want to be helpful. It just doesn't occur to them to offer something so simple because they've never been through grief.

- Who can mow your lawn, weed your garden, shovel your walks for the first and second winter (that's what you need, honestly)?
- Who has a clean house and would love to help by cleaning your house? Or doing your laundry?
- Who can pick up your kids from activities?
- Who is shopping all the time and would be happy to grab milk or eggs or toilet paper for you?

List their names, and how you know they would like to help. Do this only when you are having a decent moment or do it with a friend because your brain is functioning better at those times. Then call them and ask them if you could count on them to help in this one way.

Keep that list on your fridge or next to your phone and maybe an extra copy in your purse or wallet for those times when you are out and need help.

> Reminders can become your best friends. They help when your brain isn't fully functioning.

Know that our brains do not think clearly when we are grieving, so we don't find solutions to our problems easily. This is why I suggest you keep the list available, so you don't have to think much. Many problems often arise in the early months of grieving because the critical thinking part of our brains is not functioning fully, if at all.

3) **Set out reminders.** I have a list at www.PassingThroughGrief.com/Refrigerat orReminders. Visit the site and print out my refrigerator reminders. Post them on your refrigerator and around the house to remind you what to do. Remember, your brain is not functioning at full capacity until you begin to recover from grief. You **need**

support, but you don't remember to call friends and family. The reminder is your prompt.

4) **Take care of yourself**. The most important thing you can do in the beginning: Take care of your physical and emotional needs.
   - Make sure you drink water and rest when you can.
   - Take naps on your lunch break if you have to go back to work immediately.
   - Shut your door and tell coworkers whom you trust that you are taking a power nap. This is the most important step in the first months.

5) **Allow and welcome all the emotions**. Finally, allowing and welcoming all the emotions that show up is good for you. They are all part of you and an expression of all you are feeling. Letting them flow up and through you is healthiest for your mind and body.

The emotions can be extremely intense and like nothing you have ever felt. It can feel frightening at times. People often tell me that they felt like they were going crazy at moments. The more you can express the emotions naturally as they arise, the better your body can recover.

Summary

- Determine what you need at the moment and ask for help.
- For now, cope ... just cope. Aim to get through the next few minutes or hours or day.
- Coping is your body's natural response to loss.
- Make a list of people who can be your Be-ers and Do-ers along with the ways in which they can help you.
- Keep reminders on your fridge, by your phone, and wherever they are helpful. Remember that your brain is not functioning at full capacity. Don't rely on it.
- Take care of your own physical and emotional needs.
- Allow emotions to flow.

"We are not meant to stay wounded. We are supposed to move through our tragedies and challenges and to help each other move through the many painful episodes of our lives. By remaining stuck in the power of our wounds, we block our own transformation. We overlook the greater gifts inherent in our wounds – the strength to overcome them and the lessons that we are meant to receive through them."

~ Caroline Myss

His Death Was the Easy Part

Chapter Two:
Grief 101

"Coping is about barely holding on."

~ B.S. Allen

While coping has its initial place in the process, simply coping actually slows your recovery. Here is a very important fact to accept and understand: You are meant to *recover* after a loss and from grief.

Grief is the instinctive result of loss. It is our normal and natural response to a loss, according to The Grief Recovery Institute. However, you are meant to recover from grief and not stay stuck in grief forever.

Coping is about barely surviving.

To cope with something is to tolerate or minimize stress, solve personal problems. The combination of loss and grief is not a problem to be solved. It is not stress to simply be minimized. It is a reaction to a circumstance or experience that must be worked through and released. This is where we get stuck. This is why our grief recovery after a death of our special person is slowed or stopped completely. You and all your support systems aim to tolerate or minimize the stress of loss and grief. Yes, it is correct that loss and grief are highly stressful on our bodies and minds. But aiming to play down the stress rather than release it will not allow us to move through the grief so that we can move forward to live wholeheartedly in the future.

Dying of a Broken Heart

Grief not properly handled and continuing for a long time puts our stress level in overdrive, and we burn out, literally. Grief not properly handled is not only slowing your recovery, it is physically harming you and has proven at times to be deadly.

Grievers get sick more often, and even the common cold lasts longer. Chronic and terminal illnesses are greatly increased in widows and widowers. Studies show higher risk of accidents as well in the first year, and suicide rate among widows and widowers is increased. Dying of a broken heart is a real thing! (To learn more, see the Broken Heart Syndrome study reference in the Resource section.)

Our memory is jeopardized. Our critical thinking and planning abilities are not working. Our bodies are created to handle short bits of stress. The death of a special person in our life is a huge stressor because we are social beings. We depend on others for our survival.

This is a stress alert. Listen carefully. If you have experienced a significant death or loss of any kind in the past few years, you are most likely under a great deal of stress. Stress negatively affects our bodies if it goes on too long and is not addressed. Our bodies are wired to handle stress for short periods, not for years.

When I called for life insurance, I was told that I was at a higher risk for illness because my husband had died! I panicked. I had three young children and was now a single parent. I could not get sick. I could not die. My children needed me.

I learned why I was at a higher risk. Grief is very stressful on our bodies. It puts a great amount of strain on our cardiovascular system (heart racing in fight-or-flight state, overworking the heart), our respiratory system (breathing shallow alerting the brain that we are in danger, not getting proper oxygen in our system), our central nervous system (chemicals for emergency situations are released over stimulating nervous system, affecting memory and concentration). Our whole body is not functioning properly and at full capacity to fight off illness and accidents.

It was coming up on the first anniversary of Pete's death. I always knew stress was not good for us. We've all heard that. I was a mess and I did not have a clue what to do about it. I was barely functioning. Friends were telling me to go on anti-depressants again. My body was completely reliving the experience of the year before when Pete was in hospice, dying.

I was at the hairdresser one Saturday morning around this time. My longtime hairdresser looked uncomfortable. We used to chat the whole time she did my hair. Now I would just stare into space as she attempted small talk and I gave one-word answers. This particular day, I was having my hair colored. As I sat with my head wrapped in foils, my phone rang. It was my friend whose husband had died also of pancreatic cancer.

Her husband died just three months before my husband died. We had tried to support each other, but we were both such a mess in grief – barely keeping our noses above water, so we didn't see each other often. Yet we felt understood by each other.

The stress of grief can readily cause illness in those who are grieving.

She asked if I was sitting down. By the sound of her voice, I knew this was bad news. I walked to a corner of the salon. Karen said, "You know I've had a bad cough for a while … I just learned I have non-smoker's lung cancer that has metastasized to my brain and liver."

I was stunned, speechless, shaking.

How could this be so? How could her daughters lose their father a year ago and now have a mother with a terminal cancer? How could the universe be such a cruel place?

When Karen died, I watched her two young daughters walk up to the open casket of their mother just two years after having done the same thing for their father. I began to recall other stories of grievers subsequently battling their own health issues. This was a major turning point for me. I realized I could be a walking time bomb. When I learned how many people became ill after the death of a loved one, I stepped into high gear.

We are naturally resilient beings. We are designed to recover from even great stressors such as death. When we were created, our bodies were perfectly developed. In stressful situations, the primitive part of our brain lights up and becomes very active. Everything else shuts down. Our digestive system slows way down. No time to eat; we have to protect ourselves from the "lions and tigers and bears." We can go on less sleep. We have to stay awake to watch out for our attackers. We are hyper alert. We pick up on signals of possible attack that go unnoticed when we are not under a great deal of stress. We sense who is on our side and who is against us and dangerous for our survival. When the danger leaves and we feel safe again, our bodies return to their normal, relaxed state.

When we don't move through grief, our bodies remain in the highly stressed state, overworking all our systems for a long period of time.

Death, loss and grief are highly stressful. Those things are the figurative lions, tigers, and bears in our lives, so our brains and bodies react accordingly, always in fight-or-flight state. A loss is a trauma to our body. But ignoring the stress does not help us recover. We must instead *process* the stress caused by loss and grief. As I mentioned, it's a process you must go through, not ignore or minimize because you can't or you will never recover. Without processing it, that stress will always be with you, eating away at you ... possibly literally.

What Is Grief?

As if you don't know! If you've picked up this book, you are most likely experiencing it right now. You were never taught how to grieve. The reason for that is simple: We don't have to be taught. It is like breathing; we do it without thinking. It is like walking; when we need it, it is there. It is our companion during loss and separation from an important person in our life. And loss is inevitable in life.

Grief is there for us whenever we have a change or a loss in our life. It could be a death, divorce, a job change, a move from our home or town, a friend leaving, or graduation. Grief is there to lead us through the loss.

Grief is our completely natural and normal response to these changes and separations. Think about nature. Looking at nature is a wonderful way to understand natural responses. Think of a tree, for instance. A tree changes each season. The tree is covered with leaves in the summer. In fall, the leaves must die and fall off the tree as the tree prepares for winter and a time of dormancy. If the tree did not lose its leaves, it could not develop new leaves in the spring. No one has to teach the tree how to move through its natural process, its life cycle.

We also have to go through the natural human process for our life cycle. Loss is part of the life cycle. Cancer cells are cells that keep multiplying without dying. Healthy cells grow, live a short life, then die so new cells can grow in their place.

This is true for us as well. We are born knowing how to breathe; we are born also innately knowing how to die and how to grieve.

The problem is that most of us are told from an early age that it is not acceptable to express our true sad or angry emotions, yet they are our natural reactions in many cases. We are told from an early age that grieving, which is the normal and natural expression of the emotions associated to our loss, is not acceptable.

Change and loss are givens. They are natural parts of life. You cannot go through life without confronting change and loss many, many times. In fact, change is constant. No living thing stays the same. Life is change, and change is loss. Therefore, grief is natural since it follows change and loss.

We are given everything we need to survive and thrive. We are wired to not only survive but to thrive. Again, think of nature. Nothing in nature (in its natural state) has to learn to be something other than who and what it is.

With clients, I often use the example of the turtle. A turtle has everything it needs for survival when it hatches out of its shell into new life. It never sees its mother. It is protected and lives a long life all on its natural instincts and natural physical makeup.

Think of a tree again. An oak tree does not have to learn to be a great, big oak tree. It just is. Everything it needs to be an oak tree is within the little tiny seed – the acorn. And it thrives "behaving" naturally. A tree has what it needs to normally recover and continue to live after a treacherous storm.

> Although it's a natural process, we have "unlearned" grief and how to process loss.

The same is true for you. You possess the natural instincts and natural abilities needed to recover from the shock and horror of loss, separation, and change. However, you learned at a young age that you did not have what you needed. Somewhere along the line, by word or example, it seems we are led to believe that grief should be avoided.

You learned grieving was wrong, and you are now trying to recover from your loss with *all the wrong information* about how to do it, without naturally grieving. If you are like every client I have ever worked with, you are blaming yourself and feeling like a loser and hating yourself for not being able to "grieve properly." You are trying everything that everyone else – who knows nothing – is telling you to do, and it's not working for you. You think you are broken. Let me tell you: You are not. Yes, you are broken-hearted, but you are not broken.

If grief is the normal and natural response to loss, what is normal and natural? Well, I suggest you think of a little baby. Think of a baby that has not had time to learn from adults and society that his natural response is bad and wrong.

Babies need to eat, sleep, and be held for connection, the three essentials for their survival. Humans are social beings, so we need connection for survival. Babies will die if not touched. It is essential to their survival.

What does a baby do when her needs are not met? Think for a minute. What does a baby do when he is hungry? What does a baby do when she is overtired and needs sleep? What does a baby do if he's had enough time lying in his crib alone and wants to be picked up or held?

You got it, the baby cries. Babies express their needs through their natural response, emotion. Emotion is the body's natural response to a feeling, be it a pleasant feeling or an unpleasant feeling. Crying is not a *negative* emotion. Crying is simply an emotion. An emotion is just a strong feeling.

Webster's dictionary defines emotion as "an affective state of consciousness in which joy, sorrow, fear, hate, or the like, is experienced..." or "a conscious mental reaction (as anger or fear) subjectively experienced as strong feeling usually directed toward a specific object and typically accompanied by physiological and behavioral changes in the body." Emotion is any relatively brief conscious experience characterized by intense mental activity and a high degree of pleasure or displeasure. The Free Dictionary defines it as "a mental state that arises spontaneously rather than through conscious effort and is often accompanied by physiological changes."

"Be strong." (Translation: don't cry in front of me.)

"Get over it."

"Leave her alone, she's grieving."

"Cry alone."

These common suggestions from others are not our natural instinct. We know innately that we need others to survive, so when we have a loss and everyone leaves us alone or tells us to not express our feelings, we cannot recover. We instead *cope* with our grief. Coping means doing it alone and suffering through it, learning to manage the pain and keep it at bay.

"Don't cry, he's in a better place."

"Be strong."

When someone tells you to be strong, what are they really saying? I hear, "Don't cry" in those words.

And now you know that crying is a very normal and natural response when someone or something that was important and meaningful to us is ripped away from us. It is our body's expression of our feeling regarding our loss.

Feeling numb after the death of someone we had been close with is a normal response. Our brain protects us in the beginning from the devastating reality.

I have spoken to hundreds of grieving individuals in the early weeks and months after an important person in their life has died. The three biggest responses in those first months after the death when I ask them about what it is like for them are:

1. They feel numb (no emotional reaction, no strong feelings, and then often feel guilty about that as if I will judge them as not having loved).
2. They cry (then inevitably apologize for crying as if they are wrong for crying).
3. They question ("Could I have done something better, different, or more?" and then they proceed to feel guilty, bad or unsure of themselves).

All of these responses are normal and natural responses, but the grievers don't know that. They have not learned that numbness, crying, and questioning are all quite common. These reactions are not necessary in order to grieve, but they are common. And if we allow these responses to move through us and be expressed, we can release the stress, eventually.

We have been taught that perhaps we should have a strong reaction in the beginning if someone we were very close to died, but then we should get over it and move on about six weeks after the death of our loved one.

We are told to get out more, distract ourselves, and not to think about it, and we will feel better. These suggestions are all part of the wrong information about grief. Actually, however, it is very natural to ruminate and think extensively about what happened and about the person who died. Our brains process the change and the loss that way. We need others who will listen without judgement and advice as we think and talk about it. People close to us who will let us tell our story again and again.

Hell Wasn't Over

Growing up and until I was 45 (and still not really grown up), I knew nothing about death, loss, and grief besides experiencing the loss of my hamster, our cats, and both my grandmothers, dying in their 90s. I learned from my parents and our culture how to cope with death and loss of special people, furry friends, and important things in my life. Effectively, I had the wrong information about grief. So when my husband was diagnosed with pancreatic cancer and then when he died 19 months later, I was ill-prepared for my reaction.

I had a plan before he died. Yes, I had decided that I would grieve "appropriately" for maybe a year, then I would pick myself up, dust myself off, and get on with life. I had three young children, you see. I could not be one of those who pined over his being gone for the rest of my life. My husband told me before he died that he wanted me to go on living. He knew I was young and had a lot of years left, so he encouraged me to care for the kids first, but take care of myself also. So I had no guilt about living. I believed that life is for the living. I did not think I was supposed to give up on life because my husband had died. Intellectually, I knew all of these things.

However, when he died, I was shocked by what happened. I thought I had just been through hell watching my strong husband suffer and face his death. Hell was over… or so I thought.

The next year, though, I realize that I have more and a greater hell to come. The grief I feel for the two years following his death is something I am unprepared for and is more painful than anything I could have ever imagined.

I feel completely exhausted, drained, spent. I can barely move in the beginning. My body aches terribly in the first few months. It feels like heavy weights around my ankles dragging me down to the ground. I feel stuck.

The first anniversary of Pete's death is approaching. Has it really been a year? I thought I would be better by now. I feel worse. I am slipping, slipping back to a year ago, only this time it is more painful. My body feels like it is experiencing the loss all over again. Friends are worried and think I should go back on anti-depressants.

Two years since he died. I am crying more than ever, but always in private. I am embarrassed at this point that I am such a mess. I look good on the outside, but on the inside, I am suffering greatly. I am scared to death of my life now. I do not have a clue how to feel any different, how to "get better." My older daughter is having a very difficult time. The whole community is aware, but by this point, they do not believe it could be a result of her father's death. No one believes that her father's death two years ago could be still affecting her. They have no idea it is still affecting me. I feel lost and alone. My life is a nightmare.

I am reading every book I can find on grief and grieving. I read others' stories of loss and grief, but none of them tells me how to get better. I go to a support group, but they all seem to be stuck in grief and just talking about the pain of their loss. That doesn't feel good to me. I am giving up on life. But how can I? I have three children who are in their teens. They need their mother. They need to see me get through this so they can. I am their most important role model. I will give up on myself, but I won't give up on my children.

The reality was I didn't know *how* to grieve after my initial natural response. I started quickly to do everything I was taught incorrectly about grieving.

I didn't realize at the time what a natural response was. I didn't know what steps to take.

Case Study

I worked with a woman whose sister had died when she was in her teens. She was very close to her sister. In fact, she felt closer to her sister than to her mother when she was a teen. When her sister tragically died in a car accident, no one knew how to help this young teen to grieve. She recalled vividly her mother telling her that her sister had died and then told her to go outside so the adults could talk privately.

This teenager was left to deal with this shocking and devastating news all by herself. She held on to the pain with no understanding of how to deal with it. She did her best to bury it. It affected her life tremendously. As she got older, she developed chronic health conditions. She saw many traditional and non-traditional doctors, tried eating whole foods, exercising and yoga. Nothing helped her heal.

She was referred to me because she had turned to a hypnotist to help her, and the hypnotist sensed there was a greater issue – grief. There had never been a safe space for her to grieve, to process her fears, her anger, her despair over the tragic death of her sister. As we worked together, memories that had been covered for over 20 years began to resurface. Through our work together in a safe place, vivid memories of her sister and the events around her death resurfaced, and she was able to process all the feelings. She was amazed that all the memories were still there so many years later. By expressing her intense emotions along with her personal story, she felt lighter all these years later.

We have all learned incorrect information about grief. I thought I was prepared for grief when Pete died, only to be slapped by the harsh reality that I didn't have a clue. I was learning as I went along and didn't know that one of the first things I should have done was to forgive myself for not knowing how to grieve.

What Can You Do Now?

1) **Forgive yourself for not knowing how to grieve!** Then complete this exercise that will help you begin to understand how what you may have learned about grief is incorrect, so you can start to better comprehend loss and grief.

2) **Write down your earliest losses.** Go back as far as you can because our beliefs are mainly formed and imprinted in our brain before seven years old.

- What losses do you recall when you were a child, adolescent, and young adult?
- Did you have a pet die, a grandparent?
- Did you move and leave your home?
- Or did your best friend move away?
- Did your bike get stolen?
- Did you change schools?
- Did a friendship end or change?
- Did your parents divorce or separate?

List **all** the losses and changes that occurred that you recall before you left home. If it comes to mind, write it down no matter how insignificant it seems.

3) **Now go back and look at each loss.** Think about what you were taught about how to grieve.
   - How did your parents act and react when each loss occurred?
   - What did they say? What did they not say?
   - How did they react to your natural response (possibly crying, anger, withdrawal, confusion) to the loss or change?
   - As you look over your losses and how adults reacted, do you see a picture

emerging? Are you starting to understand how what you learned about grief is inaccurate?

4) **Post this reminder and read it daily:** I choose to forgive myself for not knowing how to grieve when _____ (my special person) died. I have done the best I know how with my present awareness. With my increased awareness, I can choose new behaviors.

Summary

- Coping is about surviving, but we are all meant to thrive. Coping has its place, but you must ultimately move on from it.
- Stress is physically hard on our bodies, and grief is one of the biggest stressors you will ever face.
- Due to long-term stress, those grieving have greater likelihood of illness and accidents.
- Grief is a natural response to loss.
- It is important to forgive yourself for not knowing how to grieve.

"Look deep into nature and then you will understand everything better."

~ Albert Einstein

Chapter Three:
One Loss, Many Losses

"If it is impossible for you to go on as you were before, so you must go on as you never have." ~ Cheryl Strayed

It's a domino effect: One major loss causes many losses, tangible and intangible, so it is impossible to get back to normal.

I thought I had been through hell watching my strong husband suffer and face his death. As I mentioned, I thought my hell ended with death. However, I discovered in the next year that I had more and a greater hell to come. The grief I felt for the two years following his death was something for which I was unprepared. It was more painful than anything I could have ever imagined.

I lost:

- Not only my husband, I lost my closest friend and my companion
- My children's father
- Their best male role model
- My daughters' protector
- My son's guide and teacher of how to be a good man
- The family disciplinarian
- My financial provider

- My talented, free and always available handyman
- My home decorator, with an amazing eye for color, style, and space
- My personal artist, who painted all the artwork in our house, took all the family photos that hung on our walls, even made much of the furniture found in our home
- My general contractor, building a good deal of the five houses we had lived in
- My gardener, landscaper and lawn mower
- Our family's comedian, bringing laughter through our home
- The glue that held us together
- My compass
- My pillar

And I learned I lost the wall I hid behind when I felt fearful. Now in my *most* fearful time, when I needed him most, he was not there.

I had also lost my faith in God during Pete's terminal illness. I didn't even have faith. No one prepared me for after death.

Everyone was helping me get through the end of Pete's life. Meals were delivered daily during the last month of his life. Drivers were arranged to drive my children to their activities. My parents, who were in their

80s, slept on our couches in the living room and family room the last month of Pete's life and were available any hour of the day or night to help me pick my husband up off the floor after one of his numerous falls in the last few weeks or get meals on the table for the family and answer the phone. Even hospice was there with nurses visiting daily and there to answer a question at a moment's notice by telephone. They became my "friends" in the last couple of months, the people who supported me and held me up most.

And Pete was there, maybe on his way out – and I thought I was preparing for that exit, but the truth was he was still physically there with me.

Yes, I had a lot of help preparing for death, and I am forever grateful for that; however, there was nothing that prepared me for after death.

Many Losses: The Domino Effect

In the case of terminal illnesses, we think we can prepare. Others think we are preparing. However, regardless of how a loss occurs, there is absolutely no way to prepare for an unknown foreign feeling.

What if you were slated to go to the moon? There is no earthly way to prepare for the sensation of weightlessness as well as the other physical aspects of the journey. Yet we've sent men to the moon.

How did we prepare them? Simulation. We replicated weightlessness, and they practiced. Practice was the solution. Correct, but who the heck is open and interested in simulating grief to prepare for it? No way, no how is that going to happen with grief.

People are actually more afraid of grief than they are of death! We see death all over the news; we love seeing death in the movies; and we eat it up. It sells out! But grief? No one wants any part of it. How many best-selling movies feature grief? So how could you possibly be prepared? You aren't. You can't be.

> *You have not suffered a single loss. Your one loss brings many other losses with it that often reveal themselves slowly, over time.*

Give yourself a break now that you realize this.

You don't know how to move through grief and back to life. Life has become a whole new life. Nothing is the same.

Remember, your friends are waiting for and believing in you to get over this loss soon. They do not understand that it is ***impossible*** to "get over this loss."

You know why? Because this one loss has caused a lot of other losses. The one loss caused a domino effect of losses, and many of those are invisible to the outside world. Very likely, you are not even conscious of them because you did not learn that a big, gigantic loss like yours creates a gazillion other cascading losses, so you are not looking for them or noticing them... until they hit you.

So let's talk about the many losses.

I've listed my many losses that I became aware of; however, I did not realize most of them until a couple years after my husband died.

I felt completely lost in my life, did not know what direction to head, and felt terrified of my possible future. I felt like I was in a forest in the middle of the night. I couldn't see a thing in front of me, behind me, below or above. Every step was frightening and uncertain. Could I survive? Could I ever find my way out? Why was there no help available now?

I had been walking through life sure that I would live my life with my husband and felt safe in that knowledge... or, as it turned out, assumption.

When we have a traumatic loss, we can lose a sense of trust. The unimaginable occurred, so we may then fear what other unimaginable events can and might occur. All things are now possible. With our one loss, we lose many things.

When your special person dies, you have to take a look at what he or she was to you in addition to being your husband, wife, mother, father, child or whatever the relationship was.

I didn't get this at all for the first few years after my husband died. I was suffering so deeply in the beginning – my body ached to hear his voice and look in his eyes, to touch his skin and to have him hold me. But I was suffering for many more reasons.

I was lost and missing my connection to my very important person. My brain was scared to death for my survival. Our primitive brain's main focus is survival. Our primitive brain also knows that we require connection with others for our survival. My primitive brain knew I was in deep trouble.

Your reaction to your special person's death is not fake. There is a physiological response. It is quite real.

Multiple Losses in One Big Loss

Three months after my husband died, it was March and spring was arriving slowly and with a lot of rain. One night there was a ferocious thunderstorm. The loud crashes of thunder and the bolts of bright lightning left the four of us in our home all feeling uncertain of our safety. We even hid in the windowless bathroom for a time, feeling safest there. But in our hearts, we all feared for our safety because our protector was gone. Our security seemed to have been ripped away from us. As hours passed, I got the kids in their beds and we all finally fell asleep. The storm subsided.

In the morning, I walked down the stairs and immediately saw water dripping in quite a steady stream from a recessed light socket in the foyer. I had no idea what to do. I couldn't figure out where it was coming from or how to stop it. I didn't know if it could cause an electrical shock or fire. I just stood there frozen with not a clue what to do. I felt scared. I felt incapable. I felt alone.

In the past, I would have yelled for my husband if I saw water running out of odd places like the light socket! I had never even seen something like this happen when he was alive. He always handled home repair issues. He loved working on houses, and he was an amazing handyman. He could fix just about anything in the house. And if he didn't know how to fix it, he wouldn't let me know. He wouldn't panic. He would confidently get to work dealing with it. He may have ripped down half the ceiling by the time I realized he didn't have a clue what he was doing. But still, I had some sense of calm that all would be okay. Not so after he died.

Now he was gone. We had never used a handyman. I didn't know any handymen, and my friends did not have handy husbands. With each similar incident, it became more real that my husband was really gone, gone for good, never coming back.

I think my children felt an intense loss of safety and security. Their dad was a big, strong, protective Paul Bunyan-type man in their eyes. My older daughter acted out how unsafe she felt after her father died. She felt lost and petrified of going on living without her father to protect her. I did not represent strength and protection to her. I represented love and nurturing. She needed to feel protected. She needed to feel safe. We all lost the person who provided our family with a sense of safety and security.

My husband was a very confident individual. I know that was one of the things that attracted me to him at first. He was forever sure of himself even when it was clear to me that he was completely wrong. Still, his sense of confidence brought me the belief that all was well. I felt confident in his conviction. Now my confidence was gone. I felt unsure of everything. I felt frozen in my steps.

My husband also was our family's financial provider. He was the breadwinner, and I had not worked full time since having our children, nor had I worked in a field that paid a salary to support four people. I lost financial security. I lost an economic life style I was accustomed to living. And I felt ashamed. I didn't want anyone to know how scared I was and how fearful I was that I might never be able to figure out how to make the level of income my husband made.

This brought us to another loss. Just one year after my husband died, I sold our large home that he had completely renovated and made ours, and I moved my family to a much smaller home across town, as people would say, "on the other side of the tracks." This loss was one that carried an intensity of emotion for which I was completely unprepared. I felt like I lost my husband all over again when I walked out of "our" house. My children were also broken-hearted all over again. They felt like I took their father away from them when I made them leave that house he had built. Friends and neighbors would try to comfort me, saying that it made sense to move to a more manageable house. "Don't you love your new home?" they'd ask with a smile. No, it was another piece of my heart ripped out of my chest.

I lost friends when my husband died. All of my friends were married, and my relationships with them were in a routine that included only occasionally seeing each other on weekends. Our relationships were set in patterns that worked well before widowhood. My husband and I always spent weekends as a family. We may have worked in the yard, run errands, gone to the kids' games, gone on a family outing, but we did not routinely spend our weekend days or many evenings with friends. We'd talk while watching our kids' sports games or get together for a party every few months, but weekly we were separate. Now I was alone. I was one adult in our home. I lost my weekend companion, my chore sharer, my friend. My friends' lives continued as usual while mine came to a sudden and complete halt.

I lost fun. I lost the sense of relaxation I used to feel in the evening after my children were in bed and my husband and I would chill either watching a movie or reading or talking and sharing a pint of Ben and Jerry's… actually he wouldn't share, we each had our own pint, but we shared the event of eating ice cream.

When I learned to look at all the losses that I had endured, I began to be a little more compassionate with myself. I began to understand the many layers of my one loss.

Case Studies

Let's look at examples of some of my clients' many losses to understand more.

I have many clients who are stuck in grief after their mothers have died. Friends and colleagues often do not understand. They think they should be over it by now. Their mother isn't suffering anymore. Or their mother was older, so what did they expect? However, grief is not about the person who died being out of pain; it is about the person now left without their special person and suffering due to the separation, loss and grief.

One client came to me a little more than two years after her mother had died. Everyone assumed she was over her mother's death by now. Mothers are supposed to die first. She was concerned because it had been two years and she was still secretly crying nightly and felt depressed. Not only was she still sobbing, she feared for her job because she couldn't concentrate at work. She knew she had made some big mistakes because of her inability to focus well and think creatively anymore. She also had to leave work earlier since her mother died. She was afraid that she only had so long before she would be demoted or worse, fired.

My client was divorced and was raising her two young children on her own. She worked full time and had a demanding career as a marketing director with a large health insurance company. Her career had been a life saver when she divorced because she could afford to raise her children on her salary alone, but her mother had also been a life saver because she stepped in and cared for her children each day as she worked long hours frequently into the evening. Her mother was also her close friend and confidante. Her mother was her biggest supporter, cheering her on and believing in her. Her father had died when she was a teen, and she and her mother had been very close ever since.

Think for a moment. What other losses may have occurred because of her one big loss, making it impossible for her to get back to normal?

This one loss, her mother's death, caused many cascading losses in her life. No wonder she was constantly crying and feeling depressed and hopeless. She lost the comfort of knowing that her children were cared for by their grandmother who loved them deeply. She lost the ability to work late and not have to get to the day care by a certain time before it closed. She lost the person who would listen to her problems and the person who shared in the joy of her children. She lost the sense of security and the sense of financial security since her job felt at risk as a result of the many losses.

She lost the ease of going on the occasional mandatory business trip. She lost her occasional weekend babysitter, so she could take an evening to herself when she felt stressed. She lost contact with most of her friends because she was now with her children every moment that she wasn't working. She lost any fun and peace in her life living under extreme daily stress.

Telling her to "keep busy" or "be strong" or "time will heal all wounds" or "keep your chin up" or "she's in a better place" did nothing to help her. In fact, it harmed her because it caused her to isolate from people even more. These statements made her feel broken and wrong and alone.

Another client found me through a friend. When hearing me speak at a conference, she thought of her dear friend who we will call Joan for this scenario. Joan's husband had died five years previously from leukemia. He had been sick on and off for four years before he contracted pneumonia and died unexpectedly. She thought he would survive. They had not talked about death. He worked up until a couple weeks before he died. She had spent years with her primary focus on caring for him. Joan worked as an administrative assistant but did not love her work, and it was not a position that required a lot of her attention. Not only that, just a year after her husband died she was laid off.

She talked to her friends about her husband and her situation all the time going over the story of what happened endless times. Her friends were tired of hearing the story and suggested she find a new interest and a new job she liked.

Permanent Change

It is impossible to "get over" your loss. Your loss has caused many other losses in your life. There is no getting back to normal. There is no getting over it. This loss was so big that you are changed permanently as a result of it.

I am not saying you will be miserable forever. I believe 100 percent that you are not put on this earth to be miserable. You were not picked out of the bunch as the one who is supposed to be unhappy for your entire life. No, I know that is not true. But you are and have been changed permanently as a result of your loss.

> *You are permanently changed. That is one of the harsh realities of loss and grief.*

The loss has changed your life forever. Now it is up to you to take the action steps to recover from the pain of the loss. You will have to consciously choose a "new" normal. What do you want that normal to be?

Think for a few minutes about your loss. I know you think about it all the time. But this time, I want you to think about it beyond the one big loss, the initial loss. Did you hear your own story in any of the stories I shared above about the many losses of mine or of my clients?

Think about Joan's story and her losses after the loss of her husband. She obviously had financial losses. Her husband earned the higher salary and then she lost her job altogether. She may have gotten a severance package, but that would not make her future secure. She would have unemployment, but that was one half her salary and would last only a few months, perhaps longer. There would also be loss of security, loss of structure to her day, loss of seeing coworkers and close friends she'd developed from work, loss of health insurance, loss of value or importance or purpose, loss of ... the list goes on.

What Can You Do Now?

1) **Set aside an hour to an hour and a half.** Get a pad of paper, a clipboard if needed, some pens, and a box of tissues. Get comfortable either at a table if that is comfortable for you, in a chair, or on your bed surrounded by pillows. You deserve to feel comforted while doing this big work.

2) **Write at the top of the page:** "My Many Losses."

3) **Now ask yourself, "What did I lose?"** Write down anything and everything that comes to mind. If it comes to mind, write it down. Use my story and those of my clients as examples. Perhaps you suffered the same subsequent losses. Perhaps yours are very different.

4) When you are finished writing, look over the list. Acknowledge all you have been through in your experience of loss. If possible, share your story of losses with a friend who can listen.

Summary

- Regardless of how a loss occurs, there is absolutely no way to prepare for an unknown foreign feeling.
- No one wants to simulate or "practice" grief, so there is no preparation for it.
- One big loss inevitably creates a cascade of many other losses.
- Losses make it impossible to "get back to normal." There is now only a "new" normal.
- Your loss has permanently changed you, and only you can determine what you want your "new" normal and direction to be.

"After climbing a great hill, one only finds that there are many more hills to climb."

~ Nelson Mandela

One Loss, Many Losses

Chapter Four:
How Not to Recover from Loss:
My Bloopers

"The thing that is really hard, and really amazing, is giving up on being perfect and beginning the work of becoming yourself."

~Anna Quindlen

Where do I even start? If I could have had someone tell me the "steps" to healing the excruciating pain I felt following the death of my husband, I would have paid a million dollars.

When I realized my desire to guide others through grief, I feared that I wasn't good enough. I doubted myself. I thought, "Who is going to pay me to help them through grief?"

I hired a business coach to help me get started. He asked me early on, "What if you had found someone who could have walked with you and guided you through your early grief after your husband died, what would you have done?"

I said in an instant, "Oh my gosh, I would have paid anything to get help moving through the worst experience of my life."

Then I thought of my life in grief. I struggled; I crawled; I hid under the covers, behind my locked door in extreme fear that I would never find my way out; I researched grief on the Internet; I read many, many books on grief; I saw therapists. And it took me *years* to find my way out.

I did it but it was not easy, and I would have done anything to have the proper help. I simply did not have a clue how to find someone who truly could help me.

The Crazy Things We'll Try to Recover from Grief

Sometimes we just have to laugh at ourselves, even in grief.

I tried. I paid a lot of money to therapists and others in an attempt to get help. It was out of sheer desperation. However, these professionals were unable to help. They hadn't been through a devastating loss, and although they had education and degrees proving their knowledge, they didn't help me get through my grief.

I felt broken. I thought if no one can help me through this, then something must be majorly wrong with me. Seriously. I was sure I was defective. I thought I was defective in many areas of my life, so why wouldn't I be defective in my ability to grieve right and move on with life after my husband died?

I started the conventional way to move through grief. When I saw my general physician and told her my husband died, she told me I needed to start taking anti-depressants. I guess I was depressed. I had been on and off anti-depressants during other rough periods of my life. Yeah … and now my husband died. It qualified as a rough period. So I listened. I thought, "Hey, half the world is on anti-depressants. They must work well."

I took the daily dose she prescribed. And still, I bawled my eyes out daily. I took the pills as I stared blankly out the kitchen window, the bedroom window, the family room window, the car window. I kept taking them through the numbness, the confusion, the memory loss, the days I stayed in bed hiding under the covers as long as the kids weren't home. Through the days I couldn't even get a shower, through the days I found myself in a heap on the floor writhing in a pain I never could have imagined existed until I experienced it firsthand. After six months on the anti-depressants and feeling worse than I had ever felt in my life, I began to wonder if they were working. I feared that perhaps I would feel worse off of them, but I couldn't believe that was possible. How could I feel any worse than I did? So I decided to stop taking them. And guess what? I felt exactly the same.

I got into therapy right away. I tried therapy on and off for the first couple of years … therapists who said they could help me with my grief. It was nice to have a place where I could cry without embarrassment and talk about everything that wasn't working in my life, but none of them helped me recover from the pain and suffering I felt.

I joined a gym and began running. I really wanted to run away, so I thought I should become a runner. But I never liked running in my life, or any exercise for that matter, so this new discipline did not last long. Instead I paid a high monthly fee, stopped going, and felt awful about myself.

I took yoga classes, which felt good. I practiced meditation, but found it close to impossible to calm my mind and body. They both helped manage some of the stress I was carrying. But while exercise, meditation, and yoga are all great, they do not heal the grief. They keep the body minimally managing the stress level.

> *It's like you are treading water. With grief, you can go right under and be unable to even get your nose above the water line. Health and wellness classes and activities help you keep your nose above the water, so you can breathe. They don't get you to shore, but they help until you get the help you need to reach the shore.*

After the conventional, normal approaches didn't work, I felt desperate. I started trying all different things to feel better. I had to hide all my efforts from others because they would think I had lost my mind. I already felt like I had lost my mind; I felt crazy and I had to hide it.

I tried EFT (Emotional Freedom Technique, a.k.a Tapping to Emotional Freedom). It was the latest trend. It was supposedly working for a lot of people – at least for losing weight, finding the perfect relationship, bringing lots of money in, and ridding old beliefs. It sounded doable for grief. Just tap. I tapped away at pressure points for a couple of months religiously, trying to tap away my pain. No success.

I paid a couple hundred dollars for an online program that would erase my underlying beliefs that were keeping me stuck and in pain. I was given lists of affirmations that I had to read aloud and then listen to a recording that would erase my old beliefs while implanting new beliefs that would make my life better, I guess. Again, I religiously did what I was told. Can't say I wasn't committed.... I was beginning to wonder if maybe I should have been "committed."

I found a past-life regression therapist. I don't even have a clue how I came across her information. I wasn't looking for such a person. It had never occurred to me to go to a past-life regression therapist. But it was going to be my ticket out of grief ... I was sure. We spent the afternoon together and through light hypnosis, she guided me in accessing one of my past lives. I learned that I lived during the Revolutionary period. Unlike in this life, in that life I was outspoken. I candidly and vehemently spoke out in public settings for civil and political rights for women. I was threatened and instructed to keep quiet, but I refused (yay me! And before women's rights, a renegade!). I was thrown in a dungeon to die. So that explained maybe why I was introverted and quiet in this life. If I wasn't suffering in grief, I may have appreciated this information, but it didn't help with my grief and my current pain.

My story may or may not resonate with you, but I suspect, since you're still reading, that it does. Most clients tell me they have tried all sorts of ways to feel better, some as crazy as mine. Maybe you didn't try as many different things – or spend as much money in the attempt – as I did. It doesn't matter.

Grief is as individual as each of us. We all move through it at different speeds and with varying levels of intensity. There are no right or wrong timelines or feelings. Things simply are. Despite that, there is a way to move through your grief. As I've said before, it is an unavoidable journey. The length of the road through your grief is not the same as mine or anyone else's, for that matter. But it is your road, and you must travel it.

My goal is to help you navigate it, so you reach your desired destination – a wholehearted life that contains purpose and joy. If you feel stuck, it's now time to move forward.

What Can You Do Now?

1) **You know grief is not funny.** I know you haven't laughed much since your loss, but laughter is proven to be healing. And finding ways to laugh while passing through grief is beneficial. Hey, grieving can take a while, so you have to live while you grieve. Laughter is an important part of life.

   Can you get together with a friend and laugh at yourselves? Can you share some of the crazy things you have done to try to feel better and laugh about it? Aim to take yourself lightly (I've never been good at it, but I have hopes for you!)

2) **Find ways to bring laughter back into your life even as you grieve.** Go to funny movies. Find YouTube videos that make you laugh. Listen to comedians. Play with little kids; they love to be silly and laugh.

3) **Keep reading this book.** You will learn steps for actually processing grief rather than just trying a ton of activities and programs that simply keep you busy but lost and still hurting.

Summary

- Chances are you are willing to do just about anything, pay any amount to get out of the pain of your loss.
- To this point, you may have tried any number of things to stop your pain and grief, and that's okay.
- Exercise, meditation, yoga, etc., are all great ways to minimize your stress, but they will not heal you.
- Grief is as individual as you are.

- To move forward in your life, you cannot avoid the journey through grief.

"You're in pretty good shape for the shape you are in."

~ Dr. Seuss

Chapter Five:
The RELIEF Process

"Opportunities to find deeper powers within ourselves come when life seems most challenging." ~ Joseph Campbell

Grief stinks. "Stinks" doesn't come anywhere close to doing it justice, nor would stronger language that's effectively synonymous with "stinks." I don't have to tell you that; you know what I mean. Grief can be the most horrible, difficult range of intense emotions. One reason is that it's not clear-cut and orderly... and specific. It does not have specific stages you can follow to move through it. And nothing has ever hurt as much as grief.

Grief stinks because it's so undependable. Grief surprises you, slaps you when you might least expect it, and shows you a side of yourself you never knew existed.

Loss stinks. Loss stinks because it reminds you constantly - constantly - that things end. That nothing, absolutely nothing, is permanent. Nothing is for sure. Everything changes. It reminds you constantly that you can't go backward. You can't ever have what you had. Even if you didn't like what you had, it still felt safer than this!

Loss stinks because there is permanency to it. You can't go back to fix regrets. It's over. There is no do over. Loss stinks because it leaves you with a gaping hole and no clear way to fill it. It says, "You can't go back, and I'm not making it easy to go forward." It says, "I took this away, and I am not going to clearly tell you how to get something better."

Loss and grief stink because everyone ignores them until they show up and throw you to the ground, and then when you feel more weak and exhausted than you ever have, you have to find your way through. No one has taught you how to because no one ever talks about loss and grief. Everyone avoids it like the plague. And now it seems you have "the plague."

> *With loss, you cannot go back. The bridge back to your previous life is washed out.*

The Good Part of Grief and Loss

The good part is ... I know you think there is no way a good part exists, and many days I still hate this good part... but the good part is that loss and grief shove you way out of your comfort zone, and since you are so far out of your comfort zone, it is a perfect time to make changes for the better in your life. You may immediately be resistant to that notion, but you know, you can't go back no matter how much you may want to.

When we are comfortable – like when you are sitting on a super comfy recliner with the remote in one hand, a bowl of popcorn on your lap, and a drink in the other hand, and your favorite show is playing back-to-back episodes, and your partner stops in to ask you if he can get you anything else … I know I am really dreaming now, but picture this kind of comfort, we are not likely to change. My scenario may not be your most comfortable one, so take a moment to think about yours. With that in mind and picturing yourself in that state, honestly ask yourself: Are you really going to make any changes in your life? Are you really going to hear that yearning in your heart to be more, to do more?

Honestly, the answer is: "No, probably not." This is why I suggest that being shoved out of your comfort zone is a good thing. It is opening a door for you to move forward, move in a new direction that you must do anyway because you can't go back. And you can move in a positive direction that creates new purpose and joy.

Six Actions for Moving through Your Loss and Beginning to Rebuild Your Life

Knowing and accepting that you can't go back, here are the actions that I took to move through my loss and grief and set myself on the path that would take me forward. These are the steps that I take clients through as well to pass through grief and reinvent their lives.

R - **Recognize** all your losses, your current thoughts and beliefs and the feelings they cause.

E - **Express** your emotions, your pain, and your whole story of loss to another who acknowledges and validates you.

L - **Let go** of your painful attachment to the past and to your sorrow.

I - **Identify**, explore, and begin to create your expanded self.

E - **Empower** yourself through new thought patterns, better feelings, and inspired actions.

F - **Find freedom** through focused steps forward to your expanded self.

So let's begin.

"It always seems impossible until it's done." ~ Nelson Mandela

Chapter Six:
The RELIEF Process: Recognize

R – Recognize all your losses, your current thoughts and beliefs and the feelings they cause.

What does grief have to do with my "current thoughts and beliefs"? Let me explain as these current thoughts and beliefs are the keys to feeling better and passing through your grief.

Remember, as we discussed in Chapter 2, grief is our normal and natural feelings and responses to a significant death or loss. Grief actually occurs whenever we have a loss of any sort, but it has a far stronger effect on us when it is a significant death or loss.

Remember the definitions of "emotions." According to Merriam-Webster dictionary, "Emotions: a conscious mental reaction (as anger or fear) subjectively experienced as strong feeling usually directed toward a specific object and typically accompanied by physiological and behavioral changes in the body."

It is a mental state that arises spontaneously without our planning it. Emotion happens spontaneously but is driven by our subconscious thoughts and beliefs.

Feelings come from our thoughts. Thoughts come from our beliefs.

So what is really happening that takes over us? That cripples us? That causes this pain?

Let's think about it. You became accustomed to having this special person around. You didn't even have to think about it. You expected to hear their voice when you walked in. In fact, your brain counted on it. It felt safe when it heard the familiar voice. You had many automatic responses. For me, when I came home from work, the first thing I did was walk over to my husband's office above the garage to say hello and briefly rehash my day. When something big happened at work or with a friend, my natural response – without thinking – was to call my husband and tell him about it. If I had a great idea, if I was sad, frustrated, hurt, my reaction without thinking was to tell my husband.

> Emotion is a mental state that arises spontaneously rather than through conscious effort and is often accompanied by physiological changes.

If I was driving and my car broke down, I knew in the back of my mind that my husband could help me. If the kids were going through anything, who would I talk to about it? You got it, my husband. After we moved into our latest house (a 105-year-old house that needed a bit of work), I recall one afternoon making cupcakes with my three pre-school-age kids and their friends. Out stumbled a mouse into the middle of the kitchen floor. And it just stood there, not looking so good ... looking like it was on its last legs. It just stood there amidst a clamoring of five little kids. I admit I didn't know what to do. Can you guess my natural instinct? Call my husband and shout, "What should I do?!" When I was offered a promotion at work, who did I want to call instantly? You get the idea, and all of these things became unconscious reactions.

When he died, I had to think more consciously to move through life in the beginning. *I had to consciously think rather than automatically respond.* My first response would be to call my husband, then I would feel like a two-by-four hit me over the head reminding me that my husband wasn't here anymore. I was jolted into my new reality. But my brain was scared to death of this new reality because the primitive part of my brain knew that what is familiar is best. The problem, of course, is that what was familiar after loss is now gone.

It doesn't matter if you were happy or unhappy in the old, familiar life, your brain knew it, so it convinced you that you were safe there. Now when you remember that you can't tell your special someone something or rely on your previous automatic reaction, your brain sends out an alert that you are now in serious danger.

Inaccurate Truths

So what do you think may happen when that special person dies? Our brain panics. It says, "Oh no, something is not good here. I am in danger. I don't hear the voice of that crucial person." When your subconscious brain turns to tell him something, the conscious part has to wake up and be alerted, "He's not here to hear what you need to say. Oh no, you are in danger. This is not familiar. Unfamiliar is always bad."

This brain reaction on overdrive is exhausting, and the reason it is so exhausting is that you normally operate daily, moment-by-moment using 90 percent of the subconscious part of your brain. It's easier. You don't have to think so much. You do things automatically. You only use your conscious part about 10 percent of the time for critical thinking, setting goals, judging results, learning new things.

When we are very young, we develop our beliefs about the world and how it operates. Then we live out our lives by the beliefs we have developed and are stored in our subconscious. We come into the world as blank slates for the most part. Then we observe the world around us and learn our "truth" about this world we live in. We mainly learn

> *Your perception of the world – your truth about it – is learned and instilled at an early age. It may or may not be accurate.*

it from our parents. They don't even have to use words. We watch them. Since we don't have a filter yet, everything they say and, even more, their actions and energy, teach us about our world. If they believe that the world is a dangerous place, our brain will pick up that as truth, and we will live as if the world is a dangerous place.

If your parents believed that as a female, you needed a male to protect you and care for you when you grew up, then you will live as if that is truth. You will not even be aware that you see the world by that instilled truth. That was my "truth." As loving as my parents were, they, by no fault of their own, believed that a woman needed a man to be safe in the world. They did not say those words exactly, but I picked up the message loud and clear. So when my husband was diagnosed with terminal cancer and I was told that he would die possibly in six months, my brain reacted with complete and utter fear. I did not realize what the fear was at that time. In fact, I did not realize for years.

I clearly remember before he died that I would be driving and would become aware for an instant that my husband was leaving me and I would be alone. I looked in the rearview mirror numerous times when driving and was shocked to see the look on my face. It was a look of utter terror. I walked around like that. I tried hard to cover it up so others wouldn't know what I was feeling, especially my children. I vividly recall my son once looking at me and a look of fear came over his face as he asked, "Mom, are you okay?" It brought me instantly to my thoughts, and I realized I was in a momentary unaware state of terror, and it showed on my face. My instilled truth was causing this unconscious terror. I had to recover from my debilitating grief in order to understand this. The subconscious part of my brain kept saying, "You are in extreme danger. You need your husband to keep you safe. He is not here. You are at risk of dying." But that was not the truth. In reality I was not in danger of dying.

You Can't Trust Your Brain

In the beginning of our grieving, we are often in too much of a state of shock to monitor our expressions. As time goes on and we reenter our environment, we start pretending we are okay and acting okay even though we are not. We try to protect ourselves by pleasing others because our brains know we need others for our survival. We don't want to lose anyone else. We have learned that others don't like us to cry and express intense emotions.

My husband was the financial provider for our family. After we had children, I worked part time in social services, facilitating programs for women on welfare. I made very little money, certainly not enough for a family to live on. My part-time position gave us the opportunity to be available for our children, with me getting them ready for school and being home again when they returned. Despite a college degree, I was working in a field that paid very little. I had no fear when my husband was alive because we had the agreement that he provided for the family financially and I provided for the family's other needs.

> When you are grieving, your brain is not very trustworthy. It shifts into survival mode.

My husband always said that he appreciated that we gave back to the world through my career, serving others in need despite its low salary. He and I felt like it was a perfect situation: We both got to do work we liked, we could live comfortably, and make the world a better place through my work.

But when we were told he would die, I was in my mid-forties. It was late to start a career that would financially support a family of four. Additionally, there were many cuts in my field, so there were not even jobs available. Without realizing it, my brain was screaming that my children and I were in extreme danger. It was saying, "You've never made money. You don't know how to make money. You are incapable of making money. You don't have experience, credentials, skills, or the intelligence to support the four of you. You all are in big trouble!"

I did not consciously hear my brain, yet what it was saying was sinking in. I did not realize that I could not trust my brain. I was frozen and crying a lot, and I felt like a train was barreling down the tracks with me tied to them and unable to get off.

I was going to die.

My brain sent other messages, too: "You don't know how to care for a house, manage finances for a family, make wise decisions about money. You've never done any of these things; therefore, I (your subconscious brain) know you can't because you haven't."

Before my husband died, I had a dream that I was alone, and I bought and beautifully decorated a home for me and my kids. I loved the way the house looked. It was beautiful and comfortable and homey. My husband had a great eye for colors and decorating, and I loved his style, but I had always felt I was horrible at it. I awoke from the dream and felt so excited. I woke my husband and said, "I'm going to be okay. I had a dream where I bought and decorated this house and it was perfect. I know I can do it because I just did it in my dream!"

It may seem silly, but it was significant for me. It was a moment when I believed I could and would survive. But then my brain and grief covered up this nugget of wisdom – this insight that came to me in a dream, and it took me quite a while to unearth it again.

For two years after my husband died, I deeply feared that I could not find my way out of this situation and out of my grief. I felt so hopeless and full of despair. I couldn't give up because I had these three children, but I had not a clue why I couldn't move on, why I couldn't get "unstuck." I felt paralyzed, lost in thick woods with no idea of north, south, east, or west. I didn't have a compass. I couldn't even see the sun. It was dark.

Can you imagine this level of fear? Is that your situation?

It wasn't until I learned about grief and received guidance to get through it that I learned that it was my thoughts and beliefs that were keeping me in fear ... keeping me stuck. I finally learned that I couldn't trust what my brain was telling me. My brain wanted the old familiar, and the old familiar was impossible. In order to survive and move forward, I had to navigate my way into the unfamiliar, quieting the part of my brain that was terrified.

I began to shine a light on my deep inner thoughts. I began to consciously examine the belief system by which I was living. When I looked long and hard within my mind, I saw why I was paralyzed: My beliefs were not aligned with what I needed and wanted to do. My beliefs were that I was incapable of getting myself out of this mess. I had been trusting my brain and the thoughts it spewed out about what I couldn't do and couldn't accomplish. It was not telling me the truth.

I have known women to quickly remarry or enter another relationship. Friends will often think, "Oh good, she is over her grief." However, the women often tell me that is not the case. They are still hurting terribly. Their actions are an attempt to stifle the fear caused by their own beliefs … what they were taught about how the world works.

The first step is to begin to shine a light on your thoughts, the beliefs you live by and the losses.

Observing our thoughts and actions is crucial to transformation and positive change. It helps us to be more conscious. We don't even have to judge our thoughts, just simply observe them. We are not aware of how unconscious we really are most of the time. Recognizing our unconsciousness by observing ourselves for a while is the beginning of change out of default mode and into conscious choices.

What Can You Do Now?

1) **Buy yourself a journal.** Something that feels good to you. Something you like to pick up and hold and look at. It will hold your story. It will hold your pain. It will hold your lost hopes, dreams, and expectations, and it will hold your *new* hopes, dreams, and expectations. It will hold for you the thought that it is time to let go and that it is time to welcome in. It will

hold where you are in the present moment, and that will change each time you write. It will lovingly hold you as you move through your grief.

2) **Begin journaling for a half hour a day if you can.** Journaling will give you an opportunity to observe your thoughts. You will write them down and be able to see what is coming out of your brain and onto paper. When you read what you've written, you will begin to recognize your beliefs, and you will begin to recognize how they may not be "truths." Through journaling, I unearthed that tiny notion I had before my husband's death – based on nothing more than a dream – that I would be okay. When I saw it on paper, I recognized and remembered it. I realized my instilled belief was not carved in stone and could be changed.

3) **Your written words will also let you observe that you are not sad every moment of every day.** This is important. Grief can cause us to forget moments we feel peace. We begin to think we were unhappy every minute. When I look over my journals, I am surprised to see I had

days and hours when I was hopeful. Days when I believed I'd be fine. Days that supported that notion I'd had but that became buried at the beginning of my grief.

4) **Your journal is the place where you can share every feeling you have without fear of rejection** and without fear that you are causing others to worry about you, stirring the fear that you will lose the people you need. It is for your eyes only, so write everything, including the good things that happen … and yes, there are good things. Writing about them will help you be more conscious of *all* of your thoughts and feelings. Your journal will hold your creation of your life going forward.

Summary

- The first step begins with recognition of how your subconscious thoughts are running amok.
- Until now, you went through most of your day on autopilot, operating without really having to think.
- Our truths are instilled in us as young children, and these truths are based on

the perception of others and may be entirely inaccurate.

- You can't trust your brain while you are grieving. It shifts into survival mode and sends messages of fear and danger around every corner.
- Shine a light on your thoughts. Observation is critical to recognition, and recognition is critical to transformation.

"You gain strength, courage, and confidence by every experience in which you really stop to look fear in the face. You are able to say to yourself, 'I lived through this horror. I can take on the next thing that comes along.'"

~ Eleanor Roosevelt

Chapter Seven:
The RELIEF Process: Express

E – Express your emotions, your pain, and your whole story to another who acknowledges and validates you.

When you shine a light on your thoughts, it can feel even more painful temporarily. I often say to clients that we are going to open the box of loss and grief wide for a little while. We are going to shine a bright flashlight in there, and we are going to bring to the surface all the thoughts and beliefs from which we are trying to hide. We are going to look hard at them because those hidden thoughts and beliefs are making it impossible to ever feel better. They are greatly affecting your life and doing so without your conscious awareness. They are revealing themselves through your horrible feelings.

Your grief will not want this. It will scream for you to shut the box tight. It will promise you that you will be better off with it closed, but you must trust me. I am not asking you to do anything that I have not done. The outcome, if you can reach within for your greatest courage, can be transformational. I am not saying it is easy, but neither is grief. Remember, you are already miserable, so it's a good time to choose to do this work.

When I was going through grief, I felt afraid to go forward, yet it was impossible to go back. It was a curse, but I also came to realize it was a blessing.

It was tempting for me to want to shut the box. Sometimes I would scream and plead, "Please don't make me do this." I was in pain, and I didn't want more pain. However, I also knew that if I shut the box, the pain would simply continue. I was unsure and there was no guarantee that opening the box would release the pain. Yes, it took courage and trust that the unknown held the key to free me. I had to trust that opening the box would, in fact, be the way to get through grief.

> *It can be exhausting to "open the box" and empty its contents, but it is far more exhausting to try to keep the lid secured.*

What I learned was that as I moved through all the junk in the box and emptied it of all its painful contents of hurt and loss from my life, I felt lighter and eventually freer. I was then able to move forward.

A client, when we first met, asked me about what I did for a living. When I told her, she thought it was the oddest type of work. She had never heard of someone helping others through grief, but she was curious. She asked me a lot of questions with an open mind. A week later, I received an email from her. She wrote that she thought she needed my services. Her father had died five years previously, and she thought maybe she hadn't moved through her grief. She shared that she's fine ... as long as no one opens the box of memories about her father. As long as no one mentions her father, she can function and cope with life. But when there's any mention of or any thought of her father, she cries.

She kept a tight lid on her box of loss and pain. It was exhausting. She was ready to take a chance to see what would happen if she went through my program. She said it was hard work, but within two months of completion she felt better. After suffering for over five years, in just two months – after opening the box and shining a light on the losses – she felt recovered from her grief. She could talk about her father, about her past without it turning to pain.

Empty the Box

If you move through the box, you can begin to empty it and you can be freed. It is best if you can do this work with another, with someone who believes in your inner strength.

It is possible to do the work through writing, but it is most effectively done in the presence of another caring person. Someone who will stay by your side when it feels too hard and will encourage you to carry on and pass to the other side as you do this deep work. We are social beings whose survival is dependent on being with others.

You are already in pain, so now is a good time to do it: Express your emotions, your pain, and your whole story to another who acknowledges and validates you. You'll never do it when life is okay, and life will never be ecstatic if you don't empty the box by telling your whole story, your past story of much loss, of great loss, and of all the pain you have endured. Many hate to hear this, but this is where we can begin to shift our thinking and acknowledge that there can be a gift in our grief. Grief is so painful that it pushes us to look for a way out.

I have a dear friend whom I have known most of my life. She knew me long before I was married, so certainly long before my husband died. She knew me when I lacked confidence, when I was depressed, when I was afraid to try something new, and long before I discovered my passion and gained a determination and drive. Long before I learned how to move forward again.

She says that in some ways she's envious. No, she does not want her husband to die or leave her, but she understands that I never would have changed my life if I had not been pushed out of my comfort zone because of my husband's death. Remember, when we're all comfy, cozy, there is no impetus to change that status quo.

At funerals, those mourning do not have any chance to tell their story. What do people focus on at a funeral or memorial? We focus on how great the person who died was. We focus on the pleasant points. And to those grieving, it feels good in the beginning to hear stories of how loved and cherished their special person was.

But soon after the death or loss, our brains begin to review the relationship without our conscious awareness ... and they think of everything. Our brains hold every past event in our lives. They don't forget anything. Nothing is ever lost deep in our minds. It is all there whether we are aware of it or not. It is there, and it brings with it all the feelings attached to the event.

All relationships have bright times and dark times. All lives have bright times and dark times. Our brains do not forget this.

Often, if we try to do the work on our own, we get stuck in the maze of our loss. We keep replaying our stories of loss and pain, but they go around and around and never get spit out. Have you ever known anyone who has told their same story endlessly?

We must allow the emotions attached to these stories to flow as we talk. There are emotions that we were taught to stuff down in our gut or in our head or wherever you happen to stuff your mental junk that you don't want to look at or let others see.

We feel everything in grief. We are a giant, open wound, and two things can happen. We can heal or we can keep the wound open, and then it festers and oozes, gets uglier and infected. This is what can happen if we don't know what to do with our grief. Time does not heal our wound. Grief, like a wound unattended or irritated and filled with "dirt" (e.g. wrong actions or no action), can get worse. On the other hand, grief, if cared for and treated properly, can heal. Yes, it takes time (and action), but it will heal. We are naturally resilient beings. We can recover from the worst of circumstances, but we need the right environment and the right care for that to happen.

Change Takes Specific, Purposeful Action

Remember in Chapter 2 we talked about the wrong information you learned? You learned to cover up your feelings and not to talk about what wasn't pleasant. Now here you are with the biggest, most unpleasant time of your entire life.

Imagine your grief is like luggage. You tried to stuff all your feelings from past losses in a duffel bag. You keep stuffing, but you don't ever empty the bag when you return home from a trip. Instead, you're trying to prepare for the next trip by continuing to stuff more into this duffel bag. So you stuff and stuff until the duffel starts bulging and bursting at the seams. The zipper starts to break, so you get bungee cords and then duct tape to hold it all in.

However, all you have to do is empty the contents. The duffel is plenty big enough for what you need now but not big enough for all the stuff from past trips. You are trying to bury the contents from past trips deep in the bag.

Then your gigantic loss occurs and creates a lot of emotions (aka the contents you're continuing to try to stuff in that duffel bag). You have tried to wrap bungee cords around it, electrical tape, rope, but this loss is too big for any of that to hold it in. Any prior losses that weren't so huge could be contained; you could stuff them in little crevices and corners of the bag. But not this one. Way too much (emotional) stuff to hide in corners. The bag bursts. And contents from all past trips in loss and grief overflow. Perhaps the emotions unexpectedly overflow at the most inopportune times, like at the grocery store in the checkout line or while teaching in front of a class. You just burst and the tears flow.

You imagine that if you try not to think about it and don't talk about it, the pain of grief eventually goes away, and you can go on and live. Not true. It stays with you in the recesses of your brain, bothering you, exhausting you, wearing you down.

That's why people say that grief never goes away; however, that does not have to be true. It is true that your memories of your special person and the events in your life never go away, but grief can take a back seat or even further back, like in the trunk. You can carry it, but it is not in the driver's seat. It doesn't drive the car. If grief stays in the driver's seat, it takes you for a long ride only through valleys of loss, sadness, and the past.

It's time to move grief to the passenger's seat. Let it ride beside you. Talk to your grief and let your grief talk to you. Decide together where you want to go and let it read the directions once you set the course. Let grief know, though, that you are in charge now. This is your life.

Grief can be a companion for a while. It can be a good companion. Grief taught me that expression of my feelings is healing and brings relief. Grief taught me to know my feelings and to use them to guide me away from what I didn't want and toward what I did want. Grief pushed me to understand life on a new realm. Grief showed me how deeply I loved when I had not realized it. Grief encouraged me to grow and expand. Working with my grief, I came to know myself and to actually love myself more than I ever had in my life.

> *You have to move grief out of the driver's seat, or you will never be able to move forward ... beyond your loss.*

I could not give grief complete control, however. I could not put grief in the driver's seat. If so, it would decide on its own that it was in control of my life and that it was here to stay. I see this occur with many who have a devastating loss. They put grief in the driver's seat.

Express the Whole Story

Companions, like grief, come for periods of our journey. The entire journey is for us alone. We come into the world alone and we leave alone. Others get to accompany us for sections. We grow as an individual from walking with others for a time and then from walking alone for a time.

It is important to do a review of your past and your relationship with the person who has died or left.

Friends have not learned that you need to review and talk about the whole story to move through your grief. Friends will often try to stay on topics that only involve the good in your relationship. Or if it was a difficult relationship, they often think that if they remind you only of what was bad about the person, you will feel relief that you no longer have to deal with the relationship. That is not true. It is crucial that you take a complete and totally honest look at your relationship.

If friends don't get this, they are not ideally suited for guiding us through our grief.

This was surprising to me.

My husband was diagnosed with pancreatic cancer and was told immediately that he had a five percent chance of living two years. We were told there was a likely chance that he would be dead within six months. My husband was not one to avoid things. So he got right to work making amends for relationships that had gone awry. He got real about what was important in his life, and he aimed to focus on his priorities and live fully in the time he had left.

I stopped working when he got sick. I cared full time for him and the kids and accompanied him to every chemo treatment, sat by his side for weeks after his 10-hour surgery, and we had lunch together every day from the time he was diagnosed until he died. We talked about everything, or so I thought.

But two years after he died, I was suffering and could not move through my grief. I learned from The Grief Recovery Institute, where I was certified as a Grief Recovery Specialist, that we need to take a complete and honest look at the whole relationship. We can't just focus on what was good, like everyone tries to do after a death.

In doing so, I discovered that I had unfinished communication with my husband. I thought I had talked with him about everything, but I discovered that actually I was trying to protect him in the end. He wanted to die peacefully, and I wanted him to die peacefully. I had to hold it together and convince him that I felt strong and could handle life without him. I was scared to death, but I wouldn't let him know that. He told me early in his illness that he was afraid I would not be okay after he died. I felt determined to convince him that I would be. I convinced him, but I was not being emotionally honest. The truth was that I was scared that I would not be able to live without him. I did not tell him that. Unfinished communication.

There were other unfinished issues I discovered when shining a light in my box of loss. I had unfinished communication even though we knew for 19 months that he was going to die.

We may have unfinished communication for a number of reasons. It is important that we don't blame ourselves or others. We just need to understand. Possibly the person could not hear what we needed to say. Maybe they weren't open to it. Maybe we didn't have a chance. We always meant to say it but never got around to it. Maybe we said it, but they didn't hear it. All of these reasons can leave us with unfinished communication. Maybe we were afraid of the outcome.

What Can You Do Now?

Remember that journal I told you to buy?

Well, now it's time to start writing again.

1) **Write each day,** for a half hour or so OR until you feel complete for that day. Tell your story up until today. Write about what happened. Allow any emotion to rise and come out as you write.

2) **It is cathartic to write and tell our stories.** It's great to tell it over and over until you feel it release. Tough if others don't want to hear it. You need to tell it. It is a way that

you love yourself back to life. I cannot tell you how long it will take or how much you have to write. Remember, grief is individual.

3) **Here are topics you may choose to write about in your journal:**
   - Write all about the big loss.
   - Write about all the losses that happened because of your big loss. (e.g. I lost my main source of income. I lost my security. I lost my children's father and main male role model.)
   - Write about what you miss.
   - Write about what you fear.
   - Write your apologies. Everything for which you want to apologize.
   - Write as if you are writing to your special person who has died. Write an apology for every fight that still plays over in your mind. Everything you said and didn't say that may have hurt them. If a regret comes to mind, then write about it in your journal.
   - Write about everything you did and didn't do that may have hurt them.
   - Write about everything they said or did or did not say or do that made you angry, made you sad, made you

resentful. Everything that hurt you intentionally or unintentionally throughout your relationship that was left unresolved when they died.

- Write in your journal everything you wish you could tell them.

Summary

- We naturally want to hide from painful emotions, but to move through grief, you must shine a light on them, emptying "the box" of its painful contents.
- Yes, it hurts, but you're already hurting and will continue to hurt until you do this.
- Loss brings with it the opportunity to redirect your life.
- Your brain likes the familiar, even if the familiar wasn't all that great or was even downright negative.
- Comfort leads to complacency, and complacency stifles growth.
- Move grief out of the driver's seat. Yes, it may ride along for a while, but you must assert control.
- Express the whole story, not just the good parts.

"There is no greater agony than bearing an untold story inside you." ~ *Maya Angelou*

Chapter Eight:
The RELIEF Process: Let Go

L – Let go of your painful attachment to
your loss, to the past and to your sorrow.

Let go. Your first thought is: "How do I do this?"

Good question.

It is very popular (and clichéd) to hear that time will heal your wound, suggesting if you just sit and wait long enough, the pain of the past event will lessen and maybe even go away. Not true. And that's not "letting go."

Perhaps you've heard that about the healing power of time. How long have you been sad and in pain? I have literally had clients who heard that, and, 40 years later, they were still in pain. I understand. I was told time would heal me. It did not. I was crying daily two years later. I had thought in a year those tears would subside ... that I would be able to get on with life and build a new life for myself and my children.

For many, the suffering gets worse as time goes on because no one wants to hear about how they are feeling years after the loss.

Time by itself will not heal the pain of your loss and grief. I promise. I have seen it thousands of times. It depends on what you do with the time that determines your ability to heal with time. And one thing you must do is make a conscious choice to recover.

It is also popular to hear if you had an extremely devastating loss that others cannot begin to imagine that you obviously will never feel better. You can never get over a loss such as that! Another notion that is not "letting go."

When I say "let go of...," it sounds as if you actually have to take action to let go of your painful attachment. And you do. And I will tell you how.

It does not mean it is easy, but it does mean you have to take action to let go of your pain. It also does not mean you let go of the memories of the past. No, just let go of the painful attachment. It does not mean you forget that it was painful, and it does not mean that you will never cry again. It does mean that the pain and suffering will go away.

There is great power in our words. In my RELIEF Process, we spend a good deal of time shining a light on our thoughts and beliefs. Our spoken words are a reflection of our inner thoughts and beliefs.

When we watch our words, we may find that we say things like:

"I will never be happy."

"I can't live without ____."

"I can't do this."

"I have the worst luck."

First of all, these statements just simply are not true. We have choice. Therefore it is important that we monitor our language and choose our words carefully. We must choose words that empower us. We don't want to beat ourselves up for saying these things (either aloud or to ourselves) or for having these thoughts. It hurts us more to be hard on ourselves. At first we must simply observe. We need to monitor how it feels in our bodies when we make these statements.

When we say words that hurt us like the examples above, we stay stuck in the pain. When our narrative about our lives or our situations is that it will never get better or we just have the worst luck in life or someone did something to us and we are victims of our situation, then we cannot let go of the pain.

It is also important to ask, "Is this really fact?" "Is it what I want to believe?" "Does it benefit me to say these words?"

Healing the pain of grief takes action. It does not simply happen if we sit by doing nothing. Remember, time by itself does not heal all wounds; it does not heal the grief wound. Healing does not happen if we take no action or the wrong action.

Words Have Power

Letting go of the pain is a conscious choice. You have to intend it and say it to have it happen. It's not that one day you wake up and the pain is gone. *You have to **decide** that you want something different.*

There are many examples that support this idea. For example, I always considered myself a poor writer. It was a narrative I carried around for most of my life until now. I was always in awe of writers, and I was very grateful for people who shared their wisdom in books. I love reading books that help me look at life from new perspectives. I love gathering new ways to expand myself.

I had trouble healing from my grief, but I finally discovered how to heal my grief, and in doing so, found new purpose and excitement about life. I literally remade my life!

I felt without a doubt that I wanted to help others to reduce their suffering. I needed to get my newfound wisdom out to the world. But I had a mental narrative that I am not a writer. Yes, I was helping people through my business, but I knew I had to write a book so that I could help even more people. My first reaction was, "I can't." I had to draw the line here because I thought myself to be a horrible writer. I could feel in my heart that I would love to write a book to get my message out and reach greater numbers of people who were grieving, but I was scared to death!

It took months and months, but I started to say, "I am not sure how I will write a book, but I would like to write a book." Then I upped it to thinking about actually writing a book. I started thinking, "Maybe I'll find a way. Maybe I could get a ghostwriter to help." The dream became more real. I took an existing book from my shelf and made a new cover for it with a title and my name as the author, and I kept it sitting on my desk in plain view. Then I got up the courage to tell friends that I was writing a book. That was the scariest aspect because I felt like an imposter. I thought, "Who do you think you are?" But I quieted that voice. When I started telling more and more people that I was writing a book, I realized **I really was writing a book!**

> *What you express, either positive or negative, tends to become your reality. Make your expressions positive ones!*

Our spoken word is extremely powerful! By telling people about writing my book, it made this dream of mine come true. I made a conscious choice to let go of the old, negative, painful belief and say what I wanted. After all, you are reading *my* book. You have no idea what a stretch and seeming impossibility this was to me at one point.

What Can You Do Now?

What can you begin to say about your life? What do you want to release from your life? What do you want to bring into your life?

1) **You have to choose.** The first step in choosing is to say it aloud and/or write it on paper. These two forms of expression begin to make it happen. You can write it or say it before you actually do it. Try writing and saying some statements about letting go of pain that can make you feel better:

   - "I am in the process of releasing my pain."
   - "I have decided to not let the pain from the past hurt me anymore."
   - "I intend to no longer view myself as a victim."
   - "I am willing to begin to release the pain of my loss and my grief."
   - "I am willing to forgive myself for all past mistakes and actions intentional and unintentional that I fear may have been harmful to another."
   - "I choose to forgive and release resentment toward everyone who has hurt me intentionally or unintentionally."

2) **Change your thoughts.** The second step is to state what you want aloud. (Look at the list of statements below.)

   Stand up.

While standing with your head held high, eyebrows raised, eyes looking up, slight smile, hands on your hips, and chest out (this pose increases confidence and improves your mood), say aloud the statements below or ones like them.

Statements:

- "I am willing to begin to imagine my life as I want it in the future."
- "I choose to honor and express my true emotions both sad and happy regardless of what others think of me."
- "I am in the process of finding ways to live again."
- "I didn't get to choose my circumstance, but I get to choose how I will react to my circumstance."
- "I am choosing to take responsibility for my life and my actions."

3) **After saying these statements aloud, stop and check in with your body.** How did it feel to say that? Did it make you want to cry? Did it feel scary or untrue? Or did it feel good … even just a bit?

4) **Continue reciting these statements while in the pose** and continue monitoring your reaction. As you continue practicing these

statements – saying them aloud – they will start to become your reality … in much the same way that me proclaiming to be writing a book led to the very thing you are reading now.

Summary

- Contrary to popular cliché, time does not heal all wounds. You have to take action, and the first action should be "letting go."
- Letting go is not forgetting. You will never forget, but in order to heal and move forward you must *let go of the pain associated with your loss.*
- Your words have incredible power. Your words set the tone for your life, so make certain your words are positive.
- As I did when I set out to write this book, affirm what you want first to yourself in thought then aloud to others who support you.

"You may have a fresh start any moment you choose, for this thing we call 'failure' is not the falling down, but the staying down." ~ Mary Pickford

Chapter Nine:
The RELIEF Process: Identify

I – Identify, explore, and begin to create your expanded self.

It was in my third year after my husband died when I learned this step. I had by this point found a program that helped me recover from the pain of my grief. I no longer was suffering. I felt at peace with the fact that my husband had died.

I did not cry anymore every time I thought of him. I could recall fond memories and smile. I could laugh about some of his qualities that drove me crazy when he was alive but that I missed after he died. I could speak of him lightly and feel no pain. I could cry when a sweet memory like a song we both loved came on the radio… and I could smile as tears rolled down my cheeks as I thought about us singing the song together with his off-key voice that he couldn't tell was off-key.

I truly knew I had recovered from the pain of my husband's death and my grief.

But I had no idea where I was going in life now that he was gone. It was a strange state to be in. I didn't know how to explain it. I was no longer sad and stuck in the pain of the past, but I was lost and scared about my future. I guess I was in limbo. I was in between two lives, my past life with my husband and my unknown future life.

I had to remake myself. I could do it intentionally this time, not by default.

I was experiencing extreme fear. I had trouble getting moving some days, procrastinated a lot, and I did not understand why.

I came to learn that my brain was in a state of fear because it thought I needed my old life to be safe. It also knew that my old life was null and void; it could no longer be. With my husband's death, my past life was impossible to recreate.

When I looked back at my thoughts and feelings in the earlier steps, I learned why I was feeling scared.

My husband earned four times what I had ever made. I had been mostly a stay-at-home mom or at least that was how I viewed myself. Now we would have zero income if I continued this way. We lost our income provider. But I didn't know what to do about it. I had never in my life made that much money and I was now in my late 40s. What was the chance I could change that around? My brain doubted my ability. Old limiting beliefs of my lack of value and abilities were ruling my ability to take action.

I didn't know what I wanted to do with my life. I knew I couldn't go back to working in social services. First of all, I didn't want to. Second, many jobs had been cut in that field, and I had been out for years, so the likelihood of me finding a job was slim. Plus, it paid very little and would not support my family.

"So what now?" I asked.

My future felt dark and dim. My 50th birthday was approaching. One sister suggested we celebrate by going to a retreat for women. I told her I was not up for it. I was in too much fear and too confused to have fun exploring purposeful work. I didn't realize that this subject was the exact cause of much of my fear.

It would be a weekend away, though. At least a time to spend with my sister and caring for myself. I had not taken any time to myself away from my children since my husband died, and we had been through a lot. I knew the self-care was a good idea. She convinced me to go.

On the first day of the retreat, the facilitator asked what we would like to get from the retreat, and she wrote each of our answers on a poster that she hung on the wall. I said, "I would like to figure out what I want to do with my life." When I said it, it sounded absurd. How would I figure out what I wanted to do with my life during a three-day retreat?

Our spoken word and our intentions are powerful. I found the answer to my question by the end of the second day. During a visualization exercise, I received my answer. I came out of the exercise and the facilitator asked how it went. I said, "Well, I discovered what I want to do. I want to help others to heal after a great loss and remake their lives."

> *Even if you don't know how to get there... yet... begin to envision where you truly want to go.*

"Fantastic!"

I replied, "Well, no, I have not figured out myself how to feel better. How can I help anyone else?"

She responded with a powerful answer, "Don't worry about it. Now that you know, the path will be revealed to you. Just stay focused on the goal, keep your feet facing in the direction of your desire, and take little steps, no matter how small, in the direction of your desire."

At the break, a psychologist approached me and asked if I would like to have dinner. She told me that her son had died tragically 20 years previously. She struggled for years to recover. She finally attended a program that helped her. She said I should go to the training and become certified to help others. The best trainers are ones who are not psychologists but rather the ones who have experienced death and loss themselves.

The path was being revealed. It continued to be revealed.

I was remaking my life. I was feeling more alive than ever. I was exhilarated and frightened at the same time.

Change is frightening. Our bodies resist it, fight change. But I had a new purpose. I had a true passion for the first time in my life.

I knew that I was on the right path. I didn't know how I would do it, but I was willing to keep taking steps forward.

Isolation Can Be an Enemy

Often when we are experiencing the pain following the death of or separation from someone we cared deeply for, we isolate. I hear this all the time from people who are grieving. They feel antisocial.

They spend most of their time alone. And it doesn't feel good.

I get it. I was there ... and I did that big time after my husband died.

The urge to isolate ourselves happens for a couple of reasons. First, we may fear being hurt more, so without realizing it, we try to protect ourselves by keeping our distance from others.

An even more common reason for isolating is that friends, family, and others don't know what to say, and they accidentally make comments that hurt or at the very least do not feel good at all, so we stay away and isolate.

Frequently those dealing with loss and death grieve alone, but unfortunately grieving alone keeps you stuck in grief and unable to recover from the pain of the loss and grief.

If you have experienced the death of or separation from someone you cared about, you are going to have to come out of hiding. It is often scary. The world can feel dangerous after a loss. You have been hurt deeply and you don't want to be hurt again. But you are hurting now, am I right?

So in order to begin to feel better, you will need to stop isolating. This will mean moving out of your comfort zone. Passing through grief requires moving out of your comfort zone, no doubt about it. I assure you, I was stepping outside of my own comfort zone when I agreed to attend that retreat with my sister!

Don't be hard on yourself. You are doing the best you know how. Love yourself for all you have done and all you have tried to recover from the pain of your loss and grief. But in order to recover, you need to do something different than you have been doing. What you have done has not worked.

How do you stop isolating when friends aren't calling, or when they call, they make inadvertently hurtful comments? How do you stop isolating when you don't know other people who would understand and validate how you feel?

Well, it may be time to meet some new people. Take a small, empowering step. Possibly take a class such as an adult learning class in your area or find a group that does an activity you like. Check out Meetup.com, a site that lets you know of loads of groups in your area for every possible interest. There are groups that meet to do yoga, hike, walk, knit; there are book groups, financial groups, networking business groups, widow groups; you name it, there is a group.

Yes, it's uncomfortable. Yes, it is out of your comfort zone. And yet, out of your comfort zone is where you will pass through your grief and remake your life. Out of your comfort zone is where all growth occurs. Out of your comfort zone is where you ultimately find freedom.

What Can You Do Now?

1) **Find at least one person who is interested in walking with you side by side.** If you do not have a friend who is right for this, then look for a coach. (You can certainly reach out to me, and we can talk about how I can walk with you and help you remake your life after loss.)

2) **Do a meditation to begin to discover the direction you want to go.**

3) **Begin to explore** options for your future. What do you like to do? What activities bring you the most happiness? What are your strong qualities? Write these in your journal.
   - Think about the times you were the happiest in your life.
   - What were you doing?
   - Where were you?
   - These answers may hold the key to the direction you should take and the path to follow.

4) **Ask yourself, "What would I like?"** You don't have to answer or have an answer immediately. Just begin by asking the

question. One day or one morning, you may awaken with an idea. Listen to ideas that arise in you. Write them in your journal even if you don't know how it will happen.

5) **Ask careful, deliberate questions that help you get what you want.** If you ask the questions to the answers you want, you will receive the answers. The questions have power. Watch how you word your questions. If you ask, "Why am I so miserable?" you will begin to see why you are so miserable. Your life will show you broken things, loneliness, people saying hurtful things, isolation, lack of money, lack of love, lack of fun. It is answering your question, saying, "See that's why you are so miserable."

If you ask the question, "Why do I love my work?" you will begin to see why you love your work. Try it; it's amazing how it works. Use your feelings as a guide to your answers. If it feels good to you, then you are on the right track!

Summary

- Your spoken word and intentions are powerful. Envision the direction you want to take in your life and your path will start to be revealed to you.
- Meditation and visualization exercises will help you envision what you truly want.
- When you are looking for answers, simply ask the question to the answer you want.
- Carefully monitor how you pose questions. Negative questions ("Why am I miserable?") bring negative thoughts and answers. Ask positive questions instead ("Why am I happy?").

"It is by going down into the abyss that we recover the treasures of life. Where you stumble, there lies your treasure." ~ Joseph Campbell

Chapter Ten:
The RELIEF Process: Empower

E – Empower yourself through new thought patterns, better feelings, and inspired actions.

As I have said before, there is no set time for moving through grief. Each of us is unique and individual, and no one can tell us what our experience in life and grief will be. Others can share their experience (as I've been sharing mine throughout the book) and we may find similarities. We may implement ideas on our journey that may or may not be helpful, but the journey is ours alone, and we must discover our way and our timing.

In the previous parts of the RELIEF Process, you have learned to look at your thoughts and your feelings. You looked at them to discover what thoughts were causing the most pain in your grief. We let our thoughts reveal all our losses. Our thoughts and feelings brought to the surface all that we miss and regret about the past and all that we fear about the future.

Now we begin to *create* the thoughts and images of what we want so that we can begin to create our new life in line with our desires.

Through my grief and in learning to pass through grief, I have learned that my body is a communicating system designed to help me know what is working for me and what is not. It communicates through how I feel. Now that I understand this, I aim to listen to it and gather the necessary information to make good choices for me.

Two Parts of You

We have two parts to ourselves. We have the "Scrutinizer" whose job it is to take data from all past experiences and use the data to keep us "safe" going forward. She (or he) operates more from fear and thinks it would be best if we kept doing what "worked" in the past. She operates on the subconscious belief system developed over our lives. She searches through her brain, remembering every event and makes the decision, "It worked well enough. You were safe, and I want you to be safe above all else. Keep doing what you have done."

Your Scrutinizer is certain that she is protecting you by causing you to avoid change.

Our Scrutinizer loves us as best as she knows how and in her own way. She does not want to navigate new waters because she sees danger in uncertainty. She likes the old, known waters. Remember, she bases everything on information from the past, stored in our brains. She gets very scared when we try something new. She screams through our fear, for example, knots in the stomach, headaches, etc. If we don't respect and listen to her, she may scream louder.

My Scrutinizer works in the form of migraine headaches that stop me in my tracks. When I start a new exercise regimen and she knows I haven't ever exercised this way before, after a week or two, she gives me a bad cold or virus, so I make sure to stop that silly new business of exercising.

Has that ever happened to you? When you try to change a habit or behavior, something happens that makes it difficult to maintain your efforts? That's your Scrutinizer trying to keep you as you were.

There is also another part of our selves. I like to call this part our Higher Self. It is the part that helps us reach our greatest dreams. She (or he) knows we have the capability to make them a reality. She does not know about limits, and she does not have access to our past and all the beliefs that we learned as young children about what we cannot do or where we cannot succeed. She lives completely in the present. Our empowered Higher Self is adventurous and excited about living a big life. She likes us to dream ... and dream big! She is a risk taker because it is not a risk to her. We cannot fail in her eyes. We just have experiences. Whatever we dream or envision, we can be. She likes to have fun. And she shows herself quietly, when we feel good. She is more like the feeling we get when we are getting on a roller coaster. We feel a fun, excited nervousness!

When you have an idea and you think, "Ohhhh, that would be soooooo amazing if I could _____ (have my own business or help millions or write a book or fly a plane or live on an island and sell my concoction or ... whatever your heart desires)," your Higher Self is saying, "Yes!"

But then do you notice how in the next second, you hear a little voice say, "Oh silly you; that has probably already been invented. Or you can't do that; you have kids to take care of. Or silly you; you aren't a writer." Well, that's your Scrutinizer trying to stop you and keep you in the safety of what you know and have done in the past.

We have to learn to work harmoniously with the two parts – the Scrutinizer and the Higher Self – to start moving in the direction we want. They both have value to us. We have to calm down the screaming, scared Scrutinizer and use it consciously.

We can do this in a few ways. We take little baby steps, so she doesn't get too scared of our new behavior that she sees as so crazy and dangerous. We also talk to her and tell her that we hear her loud and clear and we respect that she is nervous and we promise to work with her and keep her safe. When she is acknowledged, she quiets down a little.

> When your Scrutinizer and Higher Self are in harmony, you can begin creating new, positive thought patterns.

We develop new thought patterns and behaviors with our conscious self-talk. You already began to look at what you are saying to yourself in the first few steps of the RELIEF Process. Now you are observing your thoughts to create new life-long thought patterns that serve you in remaking a life that you desire after loss.

The first step is always *observation without judgment*. Just notice your thoughts. Are they positive or negative? Are they about the past, present, or future? Where do you focus your thoughts most of the time – on what you want or what you don't want?

Then see if your thoughts make you feel better or worse.

When I began to consciously observe my thoughts, I started to notice that whenever I told myself that I would never succeed, that I wasn't capable of having a business in which I impacted the way our culture viewed grief and in which I guided people through grief and on to wholehearted living, I felt horrible. It would make me cry when I thought I couldn't do anything valuable and I couldn't make my dreams a reality.

When I said to myself, "You've never made much money and you will never figure out how to make the money that you would like to live a wholehearted life," I felt scared and depressed.

When I pictured myself helping a lot of people, giving talks and workshops to large numbers of people who were so grateful for learning what I taught them, when I thought of how I helped people heal from the pain of grief and they were able to go on and live happily, I felt great inside.

Anxiety is part of your Scrutinizer, and it can be your friend or at least be a bit beneficial. Anxiety cannot take over if you acknowledge it, take a look at it, and talk to it. Find out what it wants to tell you. It is just one of your many feelings, and they are all here to help you.

As soon as we feel anxiety, it is a sign and signal for us to listen. Don't stuff it away and hide from it. We are easily tempted to blare the music to drown it out, or cover it up with food, TV, drinking, and push it away. Anxiety doesn't feel good, so the temptation is to pretend that we are not feeling it. Instead, build a relationship with it and ask it what it has to tell you.

Overcoming Anxiety and Increasing Empowerment

You can never be more courageous than when you look at your anxiety and speak to it. When you look it in the face, eye-to-eye, it begins to shrink. It is not half as powerful as you are. And when it shrinks, that is when you hear inspired action.

I faced my own anxiety. As I mentioned, I always considered myself a poor writer. I recall that I received numerous messages when I was young that I was not a good writer. I then carried that message and made it a belief about myself. It never seemed possible for me to write. My narrative (prompted by my Scrutinizer) was, "You are not a writer. You can't write." It was a narrative I carried around for most of my life ... until now. Just as I coach other people, I finally faced my anxiety, looked squarely at it, and began taking little steps to write this book, fulfilling one of the missions I set out to do. When anxiety shrank, I was inspired.

I often walk for inspiration. Walking started when my husband was diagnosed with a terminal cancer. I felt the need to move my body when I felt fearful. A year after he died, it returned. I just had to move my body. I've never liked rigorous, exhausting forms of exercise, but walking cleared my head.

I started walking to get out of fear. I would walk and consciously feel the air on my skin, consciously look around and name all the things I saw. I would listen to the sounds. This all brought me into the present moment. It relaxed me and the movement invigorated me. I'd return home calm and more able to concentrate on tasks that needed to be done.

When I started my business, I had lot of fear. I had never had my own business, and my Scrutinizer did not think it was a good idea at all. She had many panic attacks and "tantrums." When I felt frozen, I would go out for a walk. It made a difference. While walking, I would relax and then all these great ideas for moving my business forward would come to mind as I walked.

I did all sorts of things to get myself first in a place of belief in myself, then I took inspired action. Whenever I forced action based on what I thought I *should* do, it always meant more work and more stress. When I followed my body as my guide, listening to what it wanted and needed, I felt good, and ideas flowed with more ease.

Inspired actions come from us first thinking thoughts that make us feel happy. All inspiration comes from our "happy place." We find inspiration when we do things that bring us joy; then more ideas come to us.

What Can You Do Now?

1) **When you wake up, check in with how you are feeling.** Write it in your journal. The *truth* about how you feel. (I felt extreme fear for the first few years. Even after I recovered from grief, I feared my future. I wrote it down.) Then write a paragraph about how you *want* to feel.

2) **Set an alarm on your phone that rings a few times** during the day as a reminder to check in with where your thoughts are at that moment. If they're negative, see if you can shift to a more positive thought that feels better.

3) **Talk to your Scrutinizer** and tell her that you hear her, but she has to respect and trust that you are in charge. She is the part of your brain that is fearful and actually responds to your talking to her and telling her you are on it ... you got this.

4) **Use affirmations in the most effective way.** If you say the affirmation, "I am happy," your brain may say, "No, you're not." When you say, "Today, I am choosing to find things that make me happy," your brain says, "Okay, let's go look for things that make you happy."

   As I've learned from many different authors and experts, start the affirmation with...
   - I am open to...
   - I am willing...
   - I am choosing to believe...
   - I intend...
   - I love the idea...
   - I am in the process of...
        Add the word easy, fun or comfortable to the affirmation.

5) **Then test it out.** Say the affirmation and check in with your body. How does it feel to say it? You will know if there is resistance or if it feels good. Do you say, "Oh, I like that!" Or do you say, "No, that's not happening." Adjust affirmations until they feel so good that you like saying them. They bring you joy simply by saying them.

Say them whenever you think of it. Say them in front of a mirror with confidence and conviction. Say it like you know it's true.

6) **Make a recording of yourself stating all of your affirmations** and listen to them in the car, when you are walking, when you take a break at work, when you feel fear rising, as you doze off to sleep. Change your thought patterns slowly by recording over the old thought patterns you had.

Changing your thoughts is the path to empowerment. You must empower yourself in order to move through your grief and remake your wholehearted life.

7) **Ask yourself:** What can you begin to say about the life you want to create? How do

you feel when you think about these dreams for your future?

If you feel down, is it because your Scrutinizer is telling you that you can't succeed, but your Higher Self knows you can? Use your courage. Shine that light on your anxiety, then listen for the quiet inspiration beneath the noise of your Scrutinizer.

8) **What small, inspired action can you take based on what you want?**

Summary

- In the Empowerment step of the RELIEF Process, we actually begin to create the thoughts and mental images we want – positive ones that move us in the direction we want to go.
- Your Scrutinizer likes to keep the status quo. Any change is scary and should be avoided.
- Listen to your Scrutinizer when she sends her messages in the form of fear, but let her know that you're in charge and truly know what's best for you... and her.

- Your Higher Self is the part of you that dreams big and aspires to what you truly want in your life.
- It takes courage to face your anxiety, to look your scared Scrutinizer right in the eye and speak to it. It will shrink. It is not half as powerful as you are.
- The inspired action that you need to take comes from the thoughts that make you feel happy... from your empowered self.

"Character cannot be developed in ease and quiet. Only through experience of trial and suffering can the soul be strengthened, ambition inspired, and success achieved." ~ Helen Keller

Chapter Eleven:
The RELIEF Process: Freedom

F – Find freedom through focused steps
forward to your expanded self.

Finding freedom is the final step in the RELIEF Process. Again, let me reiterate that there is no specific timetable for each step. You are an individual, and you will move at the pace that is right for you.

You are doing amazing. Trust me. The fact that you *want* to change is a giant step. Our intention is key.

As I have said more than once, passing through grief takes action on your part. You will not pass through grief and move beyond the pain of loss and on to wholehearted living by sitting around and waiting for it to happen.

You cannot meditate your way to wholehearted living. You cannot think your way there. You must, at some, point take action.

Yes, action is a necessary part of creating the life you desire after loss. However, action does not have to be difficult. In fact, it is more productive with quicker, better results if it is easy. Inspired action is the key. I have found it can actually be fun. It can be exciting. It has been for me when I follow inspired action.

The key is to first envision what you want, think about it and get excited about the idea of having it, then look for signs of actions you should take to make it a reality. The right action comes from allowing our dreams – and the necessary actions to reach them – to be revealed to us through our thoughts and feelings.

After I had recovered from the pain of my grief after my husband died, I searched and discovered how to remake my life. I followed everything that I have taught in these steps.

I knew that it was important that I surround myself with people who could support my need to rebuild my life and people who understood that I was not going back to who I was prior to my husband's death. His death meant my life and I had changed permanently. It was impossible for me to go back to the old me. I now had three children to raise alone and did not have a husband as my best friend. I had to figure it all out on my own.

I felt very alone for much of my early journey after my husband died. I felt no one understood.

I desired new friends. I tried support groups, but people there all seemed to be stuck in grief and not looking toward rebuilding their lives even if the loss had been years earlier. Many people believe their lives will be sad forever. I didn't want that.

I didn't like many of the Facebook and online groups I found, either. Participants in those also seemed to stay focused on their loss and the difficult lives they now led.

My life also felt difficult, but I knew that if I stayed focused on my hard times that I would remain stuck in my hard times. I needed to keep working on changing my thinking and focusing on better feelings and on how I wanted to positively change my life.

I started taking a chance and telling friends what I was doing. I had always kept my beliefs to myself. I was introverted and always thought others would think I was weird if I shared how I was trying to change.

I wanted to create a group of friends who encouraged each other to pursue their dreams. So I would casually drop into conversations that I'd read a book on this subject, and I'd gauge my friends' reactions. Finally, I found a friend who was curious and interested in hearing more. I shared a couple books with her. She found them

> *You cannot create change with a giant leap. That is too difficult. Focus on daily small steps instead.*

fascinating, although they were completely new concepts to her. Like me, she was willing to explore more.

We started meeting once a week, reading a book and doing the exercises to change our thinking and move toward creating what we wanted. We played with these new ideas. We tried techniques for changing our thinking.

I found more friends who also were interested. Even some old friends now were interested in what I was doing to change. My friend group changed to be full of women who were positive, authentic, fun, and open to change.

I practiced meditating and visualizing as well. I aimed to have fun learning and growing. I started getting small results… but results nonetheless. My friends and I continue to meet with a focus on growing, expanding ourselves, having fun, and creating the lives we desire.

In time, I started saying out loud to friends that I wanted to help others through grief. In my visualization exercises, I pictured myself having clients, helping them move through grief, and loving my work. I envisioned people coming up to me after talks I gave and telling me how I helped them and how grateful they were. I told some friends about my daydream and how good it felt to visualize this dream.

Not long after that, my mother told me that a hospice company was coming to do a presentation at her long-term residential home. She thought maybe I'd like to join her for the talk. They were going to discuss a holistic approach to hospice, and she knew that was of interest to me. I happened to be free that day. I went.

The hospice speaker led the group in a meditation to relax. She explained that they helped hospice patients use meditation to relax and manage pain. I was excited. This was right up my alley.

As they wrapped up the presentation, she said, "We are looking for volunteers to work at our hospice." The audience reaction was, "We don't drive. We can't do that." But I knew she was speaking to me.

I felt so excited. I walked up to her and told her I would like to volunteer, and that was the start. They had me call bereaved families who had a family member who had been on hospice and died. I began talking with people who were grieving. My dream was becoming a reality.

This is the perfect example of inspired action. I imagined what I wanted, and voila, my mother calls out of the blue to invite me to the presentation; then out of the blue, the speaker asks for volunteers. And would you believe me if I told you that within a few months, one of the owners of the hospice company called me into her office and, without my ever telling her I wanted a job, offered me a paid position as bereavement coordinator? Inspired action. It's easy. It's actually fun.

> *Inspired action results from envisioning what you want and then keeping your eyes and ears open for doors opening along your path that will lead you to the life you want.*

Not only that, they asked me to speak at a workshop. Everything I imagined and started saying I wanted to do was becoming reality, and it was happening with ease.

Today, I have given many talks on grief recovery. I have led many workshops helping people understand grief and move through their grief. And I have worked with a lot of individuals to recover from their grief and remake their lives. I am living my dream!

However, this new path didn't simply "happen." I had to monitor my thoughts. I had to spend time visualizing my dreams. I had to take action when possible opportunities presented themselves. I had to go to the talk when my mother invited me. I had to walk up to the speaker afterward and tell her I wanted to volunteer. I had to keep my eyes open wide for possible doors opening along the path to my dream.

I took workshops and training that presented themselves and were aligned with my dream. I took courses on the brain and grief to understand grief more … and I loved it. The subject fascinated me. I took a year-long certification coaching course. It was a lot of work and I felt scared that I couldn't do it, but I also felt excited. I let the excitement drive me to keep taking little action steps. Small steps that led to empowerment while keeping the Scrutinizer in check.

Throughout this time, my Scrutinizer kept screaming: "I don't think you should go with your mother. Are you crazy? Why are you walking up front to volunteer? Workshops? Training? That's scary. I don't think you can do it." And with every scream from my Scrutinizer, I nudged back with my Higher Self. I didn't go from listening to a talk about hospice care to becoming a grief recovery life coach in one giant leap. I took small steps that, despite her concerns, my Scrutinizer could tolerate. It was inspired action that resulted from my visualization and directing my thoughts toward what I wanted my life to be.

Take little but daily steps no matter how small. Little, consistent steps will not cause your Scrutinizer to send you back to hiding in the closet.

Do the things that feel the most fun. Fun helps create for your scared Scrutinizer greater buy-in to this new way of living.

Case Studies

I had a client who had gone through the RELIEF Process with me. Her husband had died three years earlier. Through working together, within three months, she healed the pain of her grief and was able to talk about her husband and her past without sadness arising.

She then realized that she had loved being in a relationship and really missed that part of life. She had loved being married, and she loved her husband and the time they had together. She decided that she wanted to take a chance and look for a new relationship.

As we worked together, she became very clear about what she wanted in her next relationship. She got excited about the idea of having love again and having a companion with whom to share her life. She stayed in that "good feeling" place as much as she could for a while, using the techniques I teach. During this time, there were times when fears and her Scrutinizer would try hard to talk her out of this idea of a new relationship. "What if he dies?" it would ask.

"Your life is full with friends, your kids and your work. You don't have time for a relationship."

We continued to knock down the barriers of her negative thoughts and feelings, and I guided her to live more in the place of excitement and good feelings. She began making new friends who were also single and she shared her desire with them. She found a new interest, painting, and not knowing how that would help her find a relationship, she started spending leisure time painting and doing activities that brought her joy.

It took just about a year of focusing her thoughts and feelings, taking small but conscious action steps, stepping out of her comfort zone, and going on a bunch of dates that were not fabulous before she met a man at a friend's party who she felt excited about continuing to see.

I can't tell you the final outcome. She is not married, but she told me recently that after her husband died, she never thought she would feel the way she feels right now about this man. It's scary and she feels like she's in high school again with her first boyfriend. This time she is trusting and having fun and seeing where it goes. This was an idea she had not even considered when she came to me grieving.

What Can You Do Now?

1) **Set goals.** Write them down and read them daily. Get clear and specific about what you want.

2) **Create a vision board.** Invite a friend or two over. Have everyone bring a lot of magazines, scissors, glue, and markers, and food (we always want good food when working to change. Our bodies buy in more when we treat them well while changing!).

3) **Find a friend, new or old, who is interested in remaking her life.** Schedule to meet every week or every other week. Share your goals and find fun ways to support each other in moving forward toward your goals.

4) **Start talking to people about your desires and see where it leads.** Keep a lookout for good things to start manifesting!

5) **Most of all, bring fun into your life.** Make it your prominent intent to do what you love!

Summary

- Passing through grief takes action. You cannot meditate or think your way through it.
- The action you take does not have to be difficult. Quite the opposite: It should be inspired and fun.
- Allow your dreams to be revealed to you through your thoughts and feelings.
- Small action steps lead to empowerment and will elicit buy-in from the scared part of yourself.

"Better a diamond with a flaw than a pebble without one." ~ Chinese Proverb

Chapter Twelve:
The "Nuts and Bolts" of My Recovery from Grief

"The day came when the risk it took to remain tight in the bud was more painful than the risk it took to blossom." ~ Anais Nin

While grief and the pain of loss are highly individual, these steps – recognition, expression, letting go, identification, empowerment, and freedom – provide your map and compass to successfully move through your grief to remake your life. I encourage you to reread these chapters as often as needed to truly understand and embrace the process. Most of all, I encourage you to take the action steps offered.

That said, I also understand that things are always "easier said than done," so I'd like to share with you my secrets. Besides the six RELIEF steps, what did I do day to day to actually pass through my grief and remake my life to be a wholehearted, authentic life that I enjoy? How did I finally move through my grief? Honestly I can tell you a few things....

I Refused to Give Up

First, I never gave up and that was unusual for me. I was not a fighter by nature. I was not a go-getter, fight-till-the-end type of person prior to my husband's death. I had been a mellow, calm person; described as easy-going, although a deep thinker. Much more of a "Be-er" than a "Do-er." I always had a stack of self-help, philosophical, and spiritual books on my nightstand, and this bothered my Do-er husband. He would say, "Stop reading and start doing."

In the years after he died, while I felt so lost, I developed a determination and a drive to not only make it through my grief, but to succeed at becoming the person I always knew was hiding inside. I don't know if it came because I didn't know what else to do or if it was one of the gifts of grief for me. I developed this strength I didn't know I had by taking one step after another, day after day. I now describe myself as determined and driven. Go figure.

Practicing Mindfulness

For many years, I had been practicing meditation on and off. Yes, *practicing*... I never felt I mastered it. I practiced being in the moment more often. I practiced quieting my mind from the constant chatter. I practiced deep breathing to relax. I had no idea how it benefitted or would benefit me in my life. It never felt like I got it "right" or that meditation helped much. But who knows? My grief was an experience I never could have imagined, so while I can't say that my years of meditating helped me through my grief, in some way, I believe it was something I fell back on and something that did benefit me.

I had been trying to live in the moment, and I believe I slowly developed the ability to do that more often and with more ease as I practiced. That really became helpful when my husband was dying and after he died. The future felt terrifying. When I brought myself into the present moment, I would feel calm.

I learned that in this very moment, whatever moment it happened to be, all was okay. That fascinated me. It was only when I thought of the future and regretted the past that I felt pain. In the present, all was well.

Sitting in the chemo room next to my husband while he was being pumped with chemicals to almost kill him, all was okay. I usually read and liked what I was reading. He usually slept peacefully. All was okay.

In the moment when my husband's spirit left his body and his body was lifeless on our bed, I can tell you all was okay. I was peaceful; he was peaceful.

In one moment, after he died while I bawled my eyes out curled in a fetal position on the floor in our office, all was really okay. I was having strong, intense emotions, but honestly even in that moment, all was okay.

In the moment that I lost our biggest client and a big piece of our income ended, all was okay.

This may seem absolutely bizarre to you. I may sound crazy, but it is true for me. When I look at each moment of my life, I realize that in each singular moment, I am okay.

It is when I think about the past and my regrets and moments I have deemed sad or hurtful that I think things are not okay. It is when I start thinking about the possible future and all the bad that could possibly occur that I am not okay.

But in this moment of the present, I am okay.

This has helped me to pass through grief. It helps me today when I leave the present and worry about a potential future outcome.

In this moment, I am okay.

I Refused to Let Fear Win

Grief brought with it extreme fear for me. I had never been so afraid for my life as I was after my husband died. I felt cut off from the source that protected me and kept me safe. That was a scary place to live. Although I climbed back in bed many mornings after getting my children off to school, each day I eventually got up and took a step. I had to find a way to move beyond my fear… to become bigger than my fear.

My fight with fear was the biggest fight of my life. It tried to keep me down, and I let it do so for many weeks. But it taught me a lot and helped me grow also. As Veronica Roth put it, my fear woke me up. If it weren't for my extreme fear, I would never have gotten to where I am today.

> *"Fear doesn't shut you down, it wakes you up." ~ Veronica Roth*

I could be apathetic at times in my life. I could have trouble motivating myself to be productive. I never was able to motivate myself to really reach for a big dream before my husband died. Life was safe.

After Pete died, life was one gigantic risk. There was no escape. The risk was to take action and possibly fail or not to take action and be 100 percent guaranteed to fail. That was how I saw it. So I began to take action. I was scared to death, but I took action.

I didn't take big action. You should know me better by now since you have gotten this far in the book. I took baby steps, just concentrating on putting one foot in front of the other to start. But consistent baby steps will eventually get you there!

If you recall from the Expression step of the RELIEF Process, we talked about moving your grief out of the driver's seat. I did the same thing with fear. As Elizabeth Gilbert wrote in *Magic Creativity*, "Fear – I let it come along for the ride, but not be in the driver's seat."

I think that is what I did: I made an effort not to let fear be in the driver's seat. It was accompanying me, for sure. I felt it; I saw it there right beside me all the way through grief, but I moved it out of the driver's seat when it jumped in there.

I Thought about Where I Wanted to Go

We can't get there if we don't know where we are going. Would you get on a plane not knowing where it was headed? Probably not. Well, why do we head forward in life with no idea of where we want to go?

I was clear that there was no going back. No, the old normal was not possible. My husband had died. There was no getting back to "normal." I had to create a new normal. If we don't think about it and consciously design it, we end up with a normal we really don't like.

I knew I wanted to be deliberate in creating a future I desired. How did I do that? The first step was to decide what I wanted. I knew a lot about what I *did not* want. If you'll recall from an earlier chapter, when we focus on what we do not want, we tend to get more of exactly that – what we do not want. When we ask, "Why am I miserable?" we get the answer, and it's all negative.

Now knowing this, I practiced focusing and thinking about and looking for things I wanted. I thought about the kinds of work I wanted. I thought about the kinds of relationships I wanted. I thought about the home I wanted. I thought about the vacation I wanted. I thought about how I wanted to feel as I went through my day.

I got sidetracked – or should I say "sideswiped" – a lot and would find myself reverting back to thoughts of all I didn't want, the sadness and pain of loss. I had to continually make the effort to refocus my thoughts on what I did want. If you ask most people what they want, their immediate reply is usually to tell you what they don't want. Most people are focusing on the wrong thing, and that which gets the focus also gets the energy and the outcome.

Baby Steps and Lots of Praise

As I've been repeating to you, take baby steps and always praise yourself no matter how small the step.

Here's some great advice I picked up along the way about moving forward: "Take baby steps forward, and on bad days, at least face your feet in the direction you want to go."

I took action, but baby steps of action. I was scared, and it was fear of big action. Big action brings out our scared selves. So I took little baby steps so "scared" would not notice. I kind of snuck in the back door of change, so my scared self didn't notice.

It was baby steps when I knew I wanted to sell our house. I was in deep, deep grief at that point. It had been just under a year since Pete died. Looking back, it feels insane that I had the idea to sell the house. But I was scared of managing and paying for such a large house with a hefty mortgage. The house was over 100 years old, and although my husband had renovated it, it needed a new roof. Plus things break in all houses all the time, and it felt like way too much for me to handle on my own.

So I took little steps. I called a neighbor who was a real estate agent and talked to her. I began to tell friends that I was going to sell it. A few months later, I had a garage sale. I asked for help from friends and family. A month after that, friends came over and helped me pack stuff we didn't use.

When I wanted to meet new people, I took baby steps. I tried a support group. Didn't like it, but I praised myself when I got in the car to drive home. When I went to a new yoga class, I praised myself for going. When I gave working out an effort, I celebrated my efforts. I kept trying new things that I thought I might like. And then always praised myself for giving it a go.

I Took Choice Out of the Equation.

I thought of this often as I became determined to get through. There simply wasn't another choice. A wise and insightful minister told me more than once, "When you make a commitment, it then becomes easy." When choice is taken out of the equation, you just have to find the way.

With no choice, I knew there was no going back and I didn't have a clue of how to go forward. With there being no way to go back, I focused on finding my way forward.

Without choice, you no longer decide *if*; you focus on *how*.

This became true for me in getting through grief. I was committed to finding my way through it and on to a wholehearted life of living my purpose. At first, my commitment was to get through grief; I had no idea about my purpose. The steps became:

1) Heal grief
2) Find new purpose
3) Live purpose

Have a Reason, Hold on to the Belief

One of the reasons I didn't give up was because of my children. I am responsible. I may not do for myself, but I will do for my children. Whenever I thought of giving up, I thought of them and I kept going.

We each have to find for ourselves the thing that will keep us fighting for our lives. It will likely be different for each of us. We each have, even if it's deep within us, a big "why" that is the reason we get up every day.

In addition to my children as my reason for not giving up, there was an experience I'd had that kept coming back to me. It occurred after we received my husband's diagnosis and prognosis, and the experience carried me forward through the most trying days, weeks, and even months.

My husband always walked our children to elementary school each morning. The school was only a half mile from our house, and it was a special time for my children to spend with their father. When he was very sick after chemo and surgery, I walked them to school.

I liked that time. We would walk and talk and walking felt relaxing. One particular day, after saying goodbye to them at school, I was returning home. It was early spring, and I was wearing a jacket but could tell it was going to be a warmer day than usual. I was noticing the buds on the trees and that spring was clearly on its way. Then my mind wandered from the peaceful present moment and worry started to seep back in. I thought, "How will I make it without my husband? How will I raise the kids on my own? How will we survive without him?"

These thoughts had been regularly crossing my mind since his diagnosis, and usually I would go into a full-blown anxiety attack in which I'd have to get out of the house and drive while screaming hysterically or go for a brisk walk to blow off the fearful energy. But this time was different.

On this particular day, walking up a hill on my way home from the elementary school, I heard a voice in my head say, "There is something great out there for you. Trust."

I felt at peace. In that moment, I felt calm. I knew all would be well. I didn't know the horror and suffering I would go through. But throughout the years following my husband's death, I would recall that memory, and I would – if even for a moment – trust. I would choose to keep going forward, believing ever so slightly that there was, in fact, something great out there for me to discover.

I held on to this slightest belief. Perhaps you've heard that we need only faith the size of a mustard seed. Well, that was about the size I had. But I held onto it.

Support

I didn't do it all on my own. I had been a very introverted and private person. I had spent my life keeping problems to myself. Friends often said they knew when things were hard for me because I would disappear. I wouldn't call when times were hard, but I'd show up again when I had "figured it out" and gotten back on track.

> "Walking with a friend in the dark is better than walking alone in the light." ~ Helen Keller

This time, with the death of my husband and my subsequent grief, I had to change that behavior. I could not survive doing it all by myself.

That was one of the gifts of my grief. I learned to open up and turn to others for support. It didn't come easily and it still doesn't, but I no longer feel I am weak for asking for help. I have seen that my life has grown in wonderful ways as a result of my being honest with my struggles and calling on others when in need. They now also feel comfortable calling me when times are hard. My friendships have blossomed, and I have much richer friendships now that we support each other through hard times and celebrate the high times.

My dear friend (who I mentioned earlier having said she was not there for me nor could she face my horror, causing our friendship to become distanced) has become one of my greatest cheerleaders as I have remade my life and started my business, believing in me when I couldn't believe in myself. We have become so much closer as I shared my struggles.

Some friendships ended, a few were able to remain the same, and some were transformed, and many new, incredible friendships developed as a result of my loss and my intention to live authentically and honestly.

Surrender

Surrender. What does that mean?

For me, surrendering means letting go of my tendency to want to control my situation, to stop pushing and struggling, to trust that all will be well if I let go of control and relax into what is.

Surrendering has meant setting goals and intentions and then letting go of the outcome and believing the universe is friendly, supporting me in reaching my goals.

Yes, part of surrendering for me was having to decide that the universe is a good place and supports me if I live honestly and authentically. When I made the decision that I don't have to work so hard and struggle to live well, life began to work with more ease for me. It doesn't mean I don't take action. I must take action, but I surrender the outcome of my inspired actions.

My husband's terminal illness, death, and my grief taught me that if I surrender to what is, I get more out of the present experience.

What Can You Do Now?

1) **Take a moment and ask yourself,** "What do I want? What do I *really* want?"

2) **Write it down.** You don't have to have any idea about how you will get it. All you have

to figure out right now is exactly what you want. Let yourself daydream. Don't worry about whether you can have it or whether you deserve it. Just spend some time thinking and feeling what you want.

3) **Next, think about your big "why."** Why do you get out of bed every morning? Why do you want to create the wholehearted life you desire? Write it down.

4) **Who is your support?** Who can you turn to when you need to express what you're feeling? Keep in mind those who support you need support themselves. Expand or cultivate relationships with this mutual benefit.

5) **Explore the way you feel best.** Does meditation bring you calm or running or being with others? Look at the ways that help you feel better.

Summary

- Think about your strengths and focus on those with a determination not to give up or give in.

- When you face fear, think of it as a wake up about redirecting your thoughts or action you need to take.
- Keep in mind that every step you need to take can and should be a small one. Reward yourself for every step.
- When you remove choice from the equation, you'll find yourself focusing on how to move forward rather than if it is possible.
- Focus on the big "why" in your own life – that is the reason for you to move through your grief.
- Don't equate asking for help with weakness. You do need support … we all do!
- Let go.

"My mission in life is not merely to survive, but to thrive; and to do so with some passion, some compassion, some humor, and some style."
~ Maya Angelou

Epilogue:
Where Do You Go from Here?

"What happens to a person is less significant than what happens within him. "
~Louis L. Mann

This chapter by design is the shortest in the book because there is only one more possible action step needed to recover from grief.

Congratulations on making it through the book. I get it; this was not an easy read. No fun romance novel here. No, this was a bit of a grief relief guidebook with bits of my personal story mixed in. I hope just reading the book and learning this valuable, correct information about grief made you feel hopeful. After my initial session with most clients – before we even are into the juicy work, they almost always say they feel better already because they have renewed hope. I hope you feel this way after reading the book.

I know you are committed to change to have read this far. You are doing the best you know how. Grievers by nature work very hard to recover; however, they frequently do not have the right tools or the right support. In this book, I included crucial information and the tools in the form of actions you can take to move through grief and begin to create a new, wholehearted life for yourself. You have to find and ask for support from the right people.

As a result of my loss, learning how to move through my grief with help and remaking my life, I have transformed from a distraught, grief-stricken woman – lost and scared with little confidence in her abilities – to a determined, caring woman with clarity of life purpose and passion to serve and make a positive impact on the world. I have not completed my life's work, and I don't ever expect to because I intend to forever continue to stretch, and grow, and find new passions, living authentically all the way.

It's not easy to take the actions necessary to stretch, change, and grow. And we cannot do it alone. One of my biggest lessons in grief was learning that I had to step out of my shell to recover. One of my biggest stretches in grief was going far outside of my shell and comfort zone and not doing it alone. I began to ask for and accept help… and that was when I truly transformed my life.

I could not do it in the comfort of my home. I had to get out of what had always felt comfortable because this change was too big. I read a lot of books but found that only reading them did not help me change. I needed the support of someone who knew the way and believed in me to succeed at reaching the other side – at passing through grief. That meant hiring a good, knowledgeable coach to walk me through the valley of grief, and that is what I eventually did.

Real change takes stepping out of your comfort zone. Real change means swimming in uncertain waters. Real change means having an expert who truly knows the way to guide you and encourage you and cheer you on. You have to step out of what you have always done. If you've always tried to do it on your own, thinking that was a sign of a strong individual, you need to now question that belief. Strong is doing whatever you have to do to recover and move forward. Strong is being willing to make mistakes and stumble and fall to get where you know you are meant to be. Strong is asking for and accepting help.

So where do you go from here? If you have read the book, and the information, though new, felt true for you but you know you need guidance and support to actually move through the processes, then the next step is to reach out to me or, if not me, someone like me who has been through grief and is properly trained to help you take the steps.

If you are interested in talking and learning more about working with me, please visit my website PassingThroughGrief.com, and you can contact me from there.

I wish for you inner peace, loads of love and wholehearted living!

Natalia

Resources:

Here are a few websites regarding the research to which I've referred as well as some of the books that helped me develop my process.

Broken Heart Syndrome:
www.nhlbi.nih.gov/health/health-topics/topics/broken-heart-syndrome

"Physical Stress of Grieving" by Elizabeth Harper Neeld, Ph.D.
http://connect.legacy.com/inspire/page/show?id=1984035%3APage%3A2521)

Ann Cuddy TED Talk (regarding the power pose discussed in Ch. 8)
www.ted.com/talks/amy_cuddy_your_body_language_shapes_who_you_are

John W. James and Russell Friedman, *The Grief Recovery Handbook*, (Harper Collins Publishers, 2009)

Daniel J. Siegel, *The Developing Mind* (New York: Guilford Press, 1999)

Esther and Jerry Hicks, *Ask and It Is Given* (United States: Hay House, Inc., 2004)

Please visit my website at:

www.passingthroughgrief.com

For a helpful meditation and additional resources.

Made in the USA
Middletown, DE
20 January 2017